The Art
of the
Law School Transfer

OTHER BOOKS FROM
THE FINE PRINT PRESS

ALSO FOR THE LAW STUDENT

The Insider's Guide to Getting a Big Firm Job:
What Every Law Student Should Know About Interviewing

Later-in-Life Lawyers: Tips for the Non-Traditional
Law Student

Law School: Getting In, Getting Good, Getting the Gold

Planet Law School II: What You Need to Know (*Before* You Go)—
but Didn't Know to Ask…and No One Else Will Tell You

The Slacker's Guide to Law School: Success Without Stress

FOR THE SUMMER AND NEW ASSOCIATE

Jagged Rocks of Wisdom: Professional Advice for the New
Attorney

Jagged Rocks of Wisdom: The Contract: Mastering the Art of
Contract Drafting (forthcoming 2010)

Jagged Rocks of Wisdom: Mastering The Legal Memorandum

The Young Lawyer's Jungle Book: A Survival Guide

NON–LAW ADVENTURES

Grains of Golden Sand: Adventures in War–Torn Africa

Training Wheels for Student Leaders: A Junior Counseling
Program in Action

The Art
of the
Law School Transfer

A Guide to
Transferring Law Schools

Andrew B. Carrabis
Seth D. Haimovitch

The Fine Print Press
Honolulu

Copyright © 2010 by Andrew B. Carrabis and Seth D. Haimovitch

Published by:
The Fine Print Press, Ltd.
Honolulu, Hawaii
Website: www.fineprintpress.com
Email: info@fineprintpress.com

Library of Congress Cataloging-in-Publication Data

Carrabis, Andrew B.
    The art of the law school transfer : a guide to transferring law schools / Andrew B. Carrabis, Seth Haimovitch.
        p. cm.
    Includes bibliographical references and index.
    ISBN-13: 978-1-888960-30-3 (1-888960 : alk. paper)
    1. Law schools--United States. 2. Transfer students--United States. 3. Law schools--United States--Admission. I. Haimovitch, Seth. II. Title.
    KF285.C368 2009
    340.071'173--dc22

                                                    2009018300

Cover Design and Typesetting by Designwoerks, Wichita, Kansas.

The text face is Esprit Book, designed by Jovica Veljoviç and issued by ITC in 1985; supplemented with chapter headings in Castellar, designed by John Peters and issued by Monotype in 1957, section headings in Poppl-Laudatio, designed in 1982 by Friedrich Poppl for the H. Berthold AG Typefoundry of Berlin, and accent uses of American Typewriter, Helvetica Neue, and Law & Order.

PRINTED IN THE UNITED STATES OF AMERICA
19 18 17 16 15 14 13 12 11 10 09   10 9 8 7 6 5 4 3 2 1

CONTENTS

DEDICATION

This book is dedicated to my family, without whom I would never have made it this far in life.

To my mother Arlene and father Vincent, for their tremendous and unconditional love and support through the years.

To my brother Scott, for his continued inspiration that only a brother can provide.

And last, but certainly not least, for the continued motivation from my goddaughter Hali, without whom I would not be known as her uncle, the "famous author and lawyer."

—A.C.

This book is dedicated to my family. Without your love and support, none of this would be possible. Thank you so much Mom, Dad, and Evan for always believing in me.

—S.H.

ACKNOWLEDGEMENTS

A series of *thank yous* are due, as there were numerous contributors to this book's development and refinement. First, thank you, Ryan H. Lehrer and Nicholas C. Wittich, for helping to lay its foundation. Your insight and knowledge about the transfer process was invaluable in helping this idea come to life.

Thank you to Jake T. Henry III, Dean Robert Jerry, Dean Kari A. Mattox, Dean LeRoy Pernell, Dean Edward Tom, Dean Jason Trujillo, and the Honorable Paul G. Hyman for their input and advice regarding the transfer process.

Thank you to Professor Robert Abrams, Professor Timothy Blevins, Professor Terri Day, and Professor Carmenelisa Perez-Kudzma for all their advice and support in making this book come to life.

Thank you to Robert Brayer, Esq., Jacqueline Pace, and Neil Wehneman for their personal narratives that added so much to the real-life experiences in the law school transfer process.

Thank you also to all members and friends on the Yahoo transfer law students group. You are very much a part of this book, and your many contributions are truly appreciated.

Thank you to Anthony Fouladi, Christopher Hancock, Saberin Jamshed, Richard Karol, Michael "Greg" Kridos, Esq., Susan Ludwig, Michael Patrone, Matthew A. Petrie, Esq., Gregory Schiller, Esq., and James M. Stark, Esq. for your advice and support throughout this project. Thank you as well to Glen Stahl, Jeri Stahl, and Lauren Stahl for your help with the cover and final details.

Thank you to the law schools that participated in our survey. The answers you provided helped to shape and mold this book into its final version.

Thank you to all of our friends, professors, and staff we met during our 1L year at Florida A&M University School of Law. We will always remember our time there.

TO HARVARD I WILL GO

Many of us dream of attending a top law school. Gaining admission is extremely difficult, of course, as the competition is so fierce. If one does not perform exceptionally well when taking the LSAT and have top grades from, usually, a top undergraduate school, the chances of initial acceptance are slim.

The good news! Completing one's first year of law study can provide a "second bite" at the admissions apple, and if the application is especially well done, it *is* possible to gain admission to one's dream school. And so, if you've worked hard and your many accomplishments support it, you should follow your dreams.

This is not merely the stuff of fiction—or of fantasy. It does happen! Here is the story of a 1L student who successfully transferred to Harvard Law School. She is a dedicated student, of course, and is in addition not at all snobbish. The title of this introduction is our idea—over her hesitation, we might add—yet we thought it important to convey the potential of a transfer application.

Here is her story:

I did not begin my first year of law school thinking that I wanted to transfer; I didn't know it was an option. I loved my classmates, my professors, and my experience at my first law school. As the year went on, however, I began to feel that it wasn't the right fit for me, and for my career goals. I was attending a law school that was heavily involved with public interest law, and that is the area of legal education where the majority of the school's resources are devoted. I, on the other hand, knew before even entering law school that I wanted to practice private international law. And so, as the year went on I began to feel that I would exhaust my interests, that there weren't enough courses I really wanted to take in my area of interest, and that there were few extracurricular activities and clinical opportunities devoted to my interests.

With these thoughts in mind, I received my first semester grades and was pleasantly surprised that those hours upon hours of studying had paid off. The few friends who knew what my grades were asked whether I was going to transfer. This is when I began to consider the idea. I approached my two favorite professors to ask their advice. Did they know of past students who had applied to transfer? They were receptive and helpful, and this was a turning point for me. Both assured me that I should do what was in my own best interest, and both would help. Speaking to them helped me believe that I actually had a good chance of being accepted to some of the schools to which I applied. I had similar grades and qualifications to their former students who had transferred in the past and they believed I would realistically be a competitive candidate. This boosted my confidence and had me seriously contemplating what I would do if I was actually accepted.

Both also discussed with me many of the important things to consider when deciding to transfer. It is extremely important that the professors from whom you seek advice and recommendations have your best interests at heart and will be honest with you. Ultimately, it was these two professors (along with a third) who wrote my letters of recommendation. They were able to put me in touch with former students who had considered transferring in the past—those who decided to transfer and those who decided not to transfer. It was *very* helpful to speak with students who had recently gone through this difficult process.

Transferring is much more than simply going to a new, higher-ranked law school and having a better name on your résumé. One of the most important things to consider is what you are giving up. You will be losing the camaraderie and close friendships from your old school—there is nothing like the all-consuming first year of law school to bring people close together. You will risk losing the feeling that inevitably comes with the end of your first year—that you have survived the worst, made it through for the better, and are now able to handle law school with a bit more confidence and with a whole group of people to support you. That is not to say you won't keep in touch with friends. Inevitably you'll drift apart, however, as you experience different situations and attend different schools, particularly those friends with whom you aren't close. It's wonderful to have finally found your niche in law school and so it's worth taking into account that you'll have to start that process over again. You will have to begin the extracurricular, publication, and clinic search all over again, and in many instances you won't be allowed to join the Law Review or other publications at your new school, or there will be only one or two spots reserved for transfer students. So if it is important for you to be on Law Review, this is a serious factor to contemplate. You'll also be losing your high class rank; when you transfer your grades do not come with you. You'll start all over again and will probably never quite regain your ranking in your new school. Your ranking for your first year is by far the most important, however, unless you are applying for a special post, such as a federal clerkship, in which case first-year *and* later grades are both crucial. You will also be giving up close relationships that you may have made with professors and others at your law school, and again these personal relationships can be particularly important in applying for clerkships. I knew that I didn't want to apply for clerkships, so the concerns regarding letters of recommendation from first-year professors and rankings were not part of my decision.

For me the most difficult stage was in making the decision to apply to transfer. I didn't want my friends, colleagues, and professors to think that I was not happy or that I didn't value my experience with them. I was worried about burning bridges, so to speak. But in the end, the people with whom I was closest (I did not tell many) understood why I was applying to transfer. This is an extremely personal decision, and not everyone will understand or be supportive of it, or of you. If you decide that transferring is right for you, it will be a life-changing experience.

I chose to apply only to a few schools where I thought I would be happier and more fulfilled, and those schools that would make a big difference in my future career prospects. And if I weren't accepted as a transfer, I was still at a good law school where I was happy, even if it wasn't the perfect fit.

The most important factor in being accepted as a transfer student is your first-year grades. But there are other factors that admissions officers take into account. Because there are fewer transfer applications—and more to go on—admissions committees really do have a chance to look at more than just the "numbers": your LSAT, GPA, and undergraduate school. They look also at what kind of person you are, what your activities and interests are, and what law professors have to say about you. I've been told that letters of recommendations weigh heavily in the process and that because I was accepted as a transfer, I must have had glowing recommendations from my law professors. I did not see my letters of recommendation, but I do think that they helped differentiate me from other applicants because I had personal relationships with each, so they could write more specifically about me than the generic recommendations they might typically write.

Transfer students seem to have other credentials that differentiate them from the "ordinary" law applicant. Having a Master's degree might have helped me a bit more than it did during the initial application. My fellow transfers all seem to have in common the fact that they have gone above and beyond a bachelor's degree, whether with a higher education degree or some other intriguing activity. It might not be necessary to have a graduate degree or unique background, but I do think it gives transfer applicants an upper hand—or is part of what makes a student seek a transfer. The point is to somehow intrigue the admissions officers and make them look twice at your transfer application. Most transfer applicants will have excellent grades from their first year in law school; so what makes *you* more desirable? Make sure that you fully express yourself and make your traits, interests, experiences, and personality known in your Transfer Statement. The law schools want to know the reason that you seek to uproot yourself from your old law school—wanting to jump up to a better school in the rankings is not a good enough reason. Some want to transfer for geographical reasons, to be closer to friends and loved ones, others want to find a school that will be a better fit for their interests, and still others want to get to their dream school. The reasons are varied, but should be compelling. They should be beyond simple résumé-building.

As I wrote before, the decision whether or not to transfer is a personal one that should not be taken lightly and should be made by no one but you. Having written that, transferring has been the best decision I've ever made. I have many more opportunities to pursue my legal and non-legal interests. Transferring has already helped with my career goals: I am working at my top-choice law firm, which almost certainly wouldn't have hired me from my old law school (this is the sad reality of the legal market, particularly at firms). And overall, I fit better and am much happier at my new school.

But it has not been an entirely happy experience. I miss my old friends, colleagues, and professors. It's been harder to find my niche at my new law school: as 2Ls, everyone already has a close group of friends, usually built around their first-year experience together. So if you are considering transferring, make sure that you are willing to be outgoing to make new friends, or, if you're more introverted, that you are willing to sacrifice some of your old friendships. Luckily, most of the other transfer students are fascinating, outgoing, and equally happy to be at a new school. They are thus a natural pool for new friends. I have made wonderful friends with both transfer and non-transfer students. But it does take time, energy, and emotional fortitude to get adjusted, so be prepared to go through stages of feeling lonely, overwhelmed, and out-of-place. This is one of the effects of transferring, and one of the many reasons why it is such a personal decision. Some might justifiably feel that starting over in an entirely new and foreign environment is simply not worth transferring. For me, these were small discomforts next to the many benefits of my new law school. In sum, I couldn't be happier.

Jacqueline Pace earned a bachelor's degree in international economics from the University of Florida and a Masters of International Business from the University of Florida and the University of New South Wales in Sydney, Australia. She attended her first year of law school at American University, where she finished in the top 5% in her class of 400 students. She subsequently transferred to Harvard Law School.

1

THE TRANSFER MINDSET

Law school is unlike any academic world you have ever seen before. Old rules or tricks that worked in college are a recipe for disaster in law school. If you are reading this book before law school, concentrate on grades. This cannot be emphasized enough. Grades will be the single most important factor in whether you can transfer at all. They are the first ingredient, like the flour in baking a cake, or the tomatoes in creating a fine tomato sauce. Good grades—*great grades*—are what is needed before any other considerations are worth considering. Without the proper grades (*i.e.,* top grades), transferring to a higher-ranked law school (which is what is usually meant by students hoping to transfer law schools) is simply not an option. So, if you have transferring on your mind before you even start your first year of law school, this is your chance—and challenge.

In addition to this, you must cultivate the professional relationships with your first-year law professors, such as the writer of the prior narrative mentioned. Building these solid professional relationships—backed by those great grades—will help facilitate the process down the road when you ask for letters of recommendation.

Think to yourself, WWCD. *What Would Cardozo Do?*

Or, perhaps, WWCT. *What Would Cardozo Think?*

If you don't recognize this name, that's okay—you will soon. The point? You should create in your mind a competition between your knowledge on the subject at hand to that of Justice Cardozo. His judicial opinions range from contract cases to the famous (or infamous) *Palsgraf* case you will study in Torts. In short, you are not competing with your fellow students: that is far too low a standard. Your goal is this: you will match the best legal minds that have ever been. In all of your first-year efforts, if you hope to transfer you must keep your focus on your grades. Moreover, you must be focused on your first-year grades before you start your first-year—meaning that you simply won't accept the common "wisdom" that what's good enough for the masses is good enough for you. Your standards are higher. *What Would Cardozo Think?*

So what should you actually do to get the great grades that you are going to need to transfer? There is a long list of books about how to do well in law school. This is not one of them. This book is written to help you maneuver the transfer process assuming and after you have those great grades. In getting ready for your first year, books such as *Law School: Getting In, Getting Good, Getting the Gold* and *Planet Law School* are written to help you with law school success. There are also books on grades and law exams, but as with most things, success in exams comes mostly from doing law school right in the first place. It will do you no good to focus on "grades" if that means cutting corners or taking the easy way out and hoping for some tricks in time for law exams; in law school that is a sure route to disaster. Good grades come from knowing the law. For that reason, it is important to start early and start right. We recommend *Examples & Explanations,* the *Restatements,* and preparing for law school exams with the Law Essay Exam Writing System ("LEEWS")—in addition to lots of hard work and *lots* of practice exams.

Knowing your chances of winning in the law school transfer process—and especially if you hope to transfer significantly up the *U.S. News* rankings to a higher-ranked law school—can really only be calculated after your fall grades come out. So, while it might not seem too helpful, in a sense grades are a given: if you have great grades, you can move two spaces forward. If not, chances are you can move just one space (or maybe just sideways), if at all. We are here to help you in the process *after* grades have come out. We are here to help navigate you through the transfer process that is confusing and filled with a lack of transparency and crucial deadlines.

If your Fall grades are great, great. But—and this is important— don't let it go to your head. You still have the Spring semester ahead of you: do not be misled by Fall grades. Many, many students have fallen *very* hard when they start to coast in the Spring—assuming they've "got it made" from the Fall—while other students redouble their efforts and zoom past. Don't trip up in the Spring based on a false sense of predestined greatness from your Fall grades.

If your Fall grades are mediocre—and this is important—don't let it mess with your head. (As in…don't believe that you're a failure.) You still have the Spring semester to shine! And your grade on each Spring exam is usually 90% or so of the final grade (*i.e.,* the real grade for the course). So, to restate, do not be misled by Fall grades. If you didn't do as well as you should have, you still have a chance. You should, if anything, try harder than ever—use this as your motivation to *really* do well.

In your Spring semester, your primary focus *must* still be on grades. In fact, they must be on grades times two. It's just not possible to overstate this: if you hope to transfer—especially upwards by one or more tiers in the *U.S. News* rankings—you must, must, must have excellent grades. They are the beginning (and sometimes end) of a transfer application.

Depending upon on how well you did in the fall, you can start a proactive approach to help jumpstart the transfer process. You should begin researching transfer-friendly schools and talking with your professors. In these discussions you might bring up the possibility of a letter of recommendation—which should follow a serious, honest relationship with that professor. Do not ask a professor who probably couldn't pick you out of a line-up. It should be a professor who has been visibly impressed by you, in class and out.

You should also start working on your transfer statement, and thinking about how you will tailor each one to specific schools. (You do not write a generic transfer statement. It should be written with that law school in mind, to show why you have a serious, legitimate interest in transferring to *that* law school.)

If you want a second chance at your dream school, you should first consider whether that law school is really for you, and you for it, and whether there are any other dream schools you didn't consider before. This is a chance to re-think all of your options. After all, if you're going to all this effort—great grades, cultivating good relationships with professors, writing yet another set of packets of forms, addenda, and information for admissions committees—why not make sure you're including all of the opportunities out there?

Additionally, there is nothing wrong with getting a head start on the application process by starting to fill out (and gather information for) the transfer application forms.

Over all else, concentrate on grades. Do your very best. Just like Cardozo.

When Spring grades come out, you should actually be quite far along in navigating the transfer process. Much of your work will preferably have already been done. After Spring grades come out, you'll then need to obtain a letter of good standing and class rank to be sent to your transfer schools prior to their deadlines. Lastly, if transferring has never crossed your mind and your recently decided you want to transfer and it is now mid-May, it's still possible. While you are somewhat behind the eight ball, you will still need to follow the above steps, and this book will be even more valuable to you. So, the special considerations and needs apply to those who have prepared to transfer from day one as well as to those who only thought about it after spring grades are out. The crucial factor is that you seriously consider and follow the various issues that we'll point out. We're not special because we're writing this down. We have, however, both been through the process. We have both transferred law schools, and we have confronted the many issues we discuss … and we did so with little official help or guidance. That is the reason for this book. It is our attempt to help everyone who will attempt to do what we did.

With all that being said and understanding that high grades is the "get out of jail free" card that takes you to the law school of your dreams, do not get caught up with all the potential "What if" scenarios that might cross your mind. While it is good to have certain contingency plans in place, neither you nor we will be able to predict with any certainty where you will get into for your 2L year. You should approach this with patience and toughness, and everything will work out for the best.

NOTES FROM A VETERAN

As a way to show how much this transfer process can help—and thus why it's worth it—here are some thoughts from an attorney who, as a law student, transferred from the University of Florida to the University of California–Berkeley Boalt Hall School of Law:

Question: How influential were your long-term goals in your decision to transfer?

Answer: Very influential. I knew that transferring to Boalt would assure me the ability to practice nationally throughout my career, and that was attractive to me because of the flexibility it would afford me.

Question: Has being a transfer student affected how your peers perceive you? If so, has it been a positive or negative?

Answer: My peers in law school generally seemed to view it as a negative, though things were never said in front of me. In the professional world, my transfer status might have negatively affected my chance to find a job, although that's just speculation.

Question: Could you briefly discuss how you went about finding that first job? Were you in a different position with the firms interviewing at OCI, or was your experience more a personal issue?

Answer: My job-seeking process mirrored that of my peers, mainly consisting of on-campus interviews. Through that process, I interviewed with several large firms. I am certain that opportunity would not have been available at my original law school. I did not have any luck with those firms. Was it the result of being a transfer? Partially, perhaps. I didn't have roots in California I could point to that would have strengthened my candidacy, for one thing. Certainly it was the first question in most callbacks that I got. I wish I could say for sure that transferring played a major role in my lack of success with larger firms, but I believe that there were many factors, including my poor interview skills. Other transfer students did fine in OCI and ended up at larger firms.

Question: Has your experience as a transfer student helped you to succeed as a lawyer today? For example, did the need to meet new people help in your professional role?

Answer: It was difficult for me, partially because I was a transfer but mainly because I had moved to a part of the country where I had no family or contacts. A significant percentage of transfers to Boalt Hall came from other California schools. I don't think they were disadvantaged nearly as much as out-of-staters.

Professionally, transferring has hardly been an issue. It rarely comes up in discussions, for example, and it hasn't posed any problems for me with my current employer. At this point in my career, seven years out or so, it seems that the sum of my work experience is far more important than my schooling—though make no mistake, saying I came from Boalt is a good thing professionally and a good starting point for many conversations with clients and other attorneys.

Question: What sets transfer students apart from other students?

Answer: Two things. First, you are an outsider in a real way that never completely changes. First year is such a unique and intense experience that it tends to bind people who have gone through it together. When you enter in your second year, you miss out on that, and consequently it's harder to forge stronger relationships with the non-transfers.

Secondly, to transfer to a top school you almost without exception have to be in the top 5% of your class, which usually means you worked your ass off to get there. Someone who starts out at a place like Boalt or at another top law school carries a certain level of entitlement, I think. They know that they can rely to a certain extent on the strength of the school's name to get them a job. That tends to promote a mellower attitude among non-transfers.

Question: When asked where you go to law school do you inform the person asking that you went to UF for your first year and transferred to UC-Berkeley your second year or do you just say you went to UC-Berkeley?

Answer: I say only UC-Berkeley, but honestly, it's more because it's easier to explain than anything else. It's really all the information most people are interested in, in my opinion.

Question: Compared with others who graduated with you, was it more difficult to find your first job out of law school because you were a transfer student?

Answer: I had a difficult time finding my first job out of law school compared to others in the class. I suppose the transfer could have been a factor, but I just don't think I had quality interview skills back then, and I also didn't really know what I wanted in a job. There were other transfers who did very well in OCI.

Question: What was the biggest advantage of being a transfer student at UC-Berkeley? The biggest disadvantage?

Answer: The biggest advantage is the access to professors you just would never find outside a Top 10 school. While the majority of instruction was comparable, there were occasional instructors who were just plain brilliant and who inspired and challenged me in a way that few others had before. The biggest disadvantage was in always being (or at least feeling like) an outsider to the law school community.

Question: If you had to do it all over again would you?

Answer: Without question. I would, of course, do some things differently, but Boalt Hall was a fabulous opportunity that got me a first-class legal education and the ability to live and work somewhere amazing I might never otherwise have had the chance to do.

Robert Brayer completed his 1L year ranked fourth out of 200 students at the University of Florida Levin College of Law. He subsequently transferred to the University of California–Berkeley (Boalt Hall) School of Law, where he received his J.D. in 2002. He practices law with Haberbush and Associates in Long Beach, California, where he focuses in bankruptcy and general business litigation.

2

SOMETHING TO GAIN, SOMETHING TO LOSE: SHOULD I LEAVE IF I CAN?

The decision to leave one's law school for a new one—magical opportunities seen hanging in the air seemingly like a glittering Disney cartoon—is possibly the most difficult and most poorly considered part in the transfer process. Here we discuss this hugely important aspect of your decision: weighing the real advantages and soon-to-be-real disadvantages of transferring law schools.

Transferring will be a simultaneously thrilling and terrifying time. There are obvious and comforting reasons to stay at one's original 1L law school; likewise there are serious reasons to accept a transfer as a 2L with advanced standing at your new law school. Like everything else we learn in law school, there is a totality of circumstance—a confluence of factors—and we employ whatever balancing tests we can construct to weigh the many variables (including highly subjective ones) to derive a binary, Yes/No, Stay/Go decision. Yet deciding whether to stay or leave requires exactly that: that you make a decision, and then that you follow through with the many details we will discuss.

For simplicity, we will refer to your original 1L law school as your "Original 1L School" and your new potential 2L law school to which you might transfer as your "New 2L School." Not terribly original, we admit, but we want to avoid confusion.

THE GRASS IS GREENER ON THE OTHER SIDE…OR IS IT?

Transferring to a higher-ranked law school is an achievement, comparable to having been admitted there as a 1L. With such an achievement comes obvious perks and privileges. In general, transferring to a higher-ranked law school will give you the benefits of a more prestigious reputation than your Original 1L School. For many, of course, this means a job. Not just any job, but a *great* job. If you are interested in a big firm job (or in a high-profile clerkship or agency job), the value of your New 2L School is substantial. Among other things, it comes with an increased alumni base and enhanced networking opportunities, and much greater "pull" among hiring partners. More legal employers hire graduates from higher-ranked law schools, and even more legal employers will consider graduates from such a law school, now and in the future. This in turn yields more job prospects upon graduation and beyond. If you are interested in clerkships, perhaps as a prelude to teaching or a specialized career, your New 2L School can not only give you more credibility, it can often be its own key to another set of binary, Yes/No career gates. In other words, chances are you might get a prestigious job or clerkship from your New 2L School that you would never be offered if still at your Original 1L School. This might seem unfair, but it is a consideration … and it is a prime driver for many transfer students.

Outside of job prospects, your New 2L School might well give you more of an intellectual challenge, with a more scholarly faculty focused in more research projects, and superior facilities (libraries, clinics, high-profile guest lecturers, etc.). As a double-edged sword, this comes with increased competition from classmates. This facilitates the learning process as you'll be challenged more than ever, but on the other side you might suffer as more of a little-fish-big-pond in your New 2L School than you were as a big-fish-little-pond in your Original 1L School. This depends on which fish you prefer to be and which pond you prefer to be in (and from).

Notably, law schools that are highly ranked tend to run a higher grade curve because they do not have to worry about bar passage rates as much as lower-ranked schools. For instance, a Tier 4 (T4) law school may run a 2.2 curve while a Tier 1 (T1) law school may run a 3.1 curve. In its most simple terms, if you "ride the curve" and sit in the middle of the class at the T4 school, you'll have grades of C's and C+'s. At the T1 school, in contrast, you might receive B's and B+'s.

Furthermore, it is vitally important to determine if your New 2L School is in a job market in which you want to practice. This is crucially important with one possible exception: if your New 2L School is a Top 14 law school. The law schools ranked in the Top 14 (T14) are deemed to be "national law schools," meaning that going to one of these schools will most likely provide you with an opportunity to practice law anywhere in the country you desire based almost solely on the name recognition of that law school. Law schools ranked below the Top 14 but in the Top 25 are considered quasi-national law schools. Their clout is considerable, but even in a law school ranked 15-25, you'll have a challenge to find a job outside that law school's natural market. For example, if you absolutely know that you want to practice in Illinois, you need not be so concerned if you transfer to a well-regarded law school in Illinois (T1 or T2) or to a T14 law school outside Illinois, but be careful before transferring to a law school even if it's ranked 15-25 (much less, 15-50) if it's outside Illinois. If recruiters from Illinois don't *regularly* recruit at and hire from that law school, you'll have a relatively difficult time landing a job in Illinois from that school, regardless of its status as a "Tier 1 law school."

Okay, so we all know of the limitless potentials of attending a new, higher-ranked school. Pay particular attention, however, to this next statement: When you transfer law schools, you lose your grades and class rank. Your *credits* will transfer—well, most of them will, as we'll explain a bit later—but your *grades* convert to Pass or Satisfactory, and you start your New 2L School with a 0.00 GPA. Next, you will almost certainly not receive a scholarship to transfer to your New 2L School. You have a better chance playing the lottery. You get to transfer to a new school; the law school gets full tuition. Both sides win. (In theory at least.)

Now to more good news: if your New 2L School is private and your Original 1L School is public, or if your New 2L School will consider you an out-of-state student while you were in-state previously, you will face a higher tuition bill. If money is no object, then disregard this tidbit (and just about every other tidbit), as you don't live in our reality. However, for the rest of us without that limitless Black American Express credit card, money is a vital issue. Private or out-of-state tuition can run (as of this writing) from $30,000 to $45,000 for tuition alone. There aren't many who have that kind of spare change in their back pockets (or anywhere else for that matter). Additionally, you will likely need to take out supplemental loans just for bare living expenses. Going to a private law school, with living expenses, can easily run $60,000 per year. Proceed with caution.

This might seem like some minor point—of course you'll be able to figure out how to pay for it!—but it is not minor. Unless you are nearly guaranteed a better set of career options with your transfer, think very, very carefully about this point: money does not, in fact, grow on trees.

Since you transfer only your credits and not your actual grades, transfer students will most likely not be allowed to apply for scholarships until after you complete at least one semester at your New 2L School. You might qualify for need-based loans, but you'll need to check specifically and carefully with the financial aid office, and you'll need to be certain you file any changes to your status as early as possible, so as not to miss any deadlines (strict or informal, as many funds run out quickly, regardless of the "official" deadline). You'll thus need to be careful about the financial aid aspect of the transfer. While much of financial aid is federally-based, not all aspects are (and many schools have other sources of financial aid funding), so again, be alert to this.

STILL MORE ...

Those grade-on law review offers you would enjoy at your Original 1L School are gone. All gone. Some law schools, like Florida State University for example, might accept a grade-on to some journals, but they are the exception proving the rule. For the most part you will have to try to "write on" to law review or journals through a write-on competition held in the summer. If so, you'll need to decide whether that is important (it is), and then be sure not to miss the competition and deadline(s). At the very least, this will add an additional load that you would otherwise not face.

Unlike "grading on"—which is based on your first-year grades—writing on to law review usually entails writing a case comment on cases and other sources assigned by that law review (and sometimes by the journals collectively). The research is provided for you, and this is nearly always a "closed universe" competition: you *cannot* refer to any other sources. The journals do this to level the playing field so everyone in the competition has the same materials, and thus the same basis to write a great (or not-so-great) comment. The write-on competition process is thus more about *how you write* than what research you can find. That written, the journals will provide exact details on how they would like the case comment to be written. Follow these instructions exactly. Precisely. Painstakingly. Do not deviate, even a little. If you have a real question about the process, then ask. Otherwise, do *exactly* what and as they say. To do otherwise is to all-but-guarantee that you will not be selected.

A case comment is somewhat different than law school persuasive writing. It is more akin to a memorandum of law where you analyze both sides of the case, objectively, and cite that case or statute that applies to that point. Like the rest of law school, there is not a "correct answer" in a case comment. You need to write objectively, clearly, succinctly, and logically. You do *not* write passionately, as a partisan, or in any quirky way. All it takes is one reader who does not like what you write to kill your chances. Think of how you would write a memorandum to the most senior partner in the most stuffy law firm you can imagine. That's how you write your write-on essay.

Make sure your writing is absolutely perfect, of course, and that your comment flows with logical analysis. The board of the law review (those voted to run it for a year), or several boards if it's run jointly by multiple journals, will review the case comments submitted and select the best ones for offers of admission. Often, the best case comment will be published in the journal.

I was accepted to Florida State University (FSU) as a transfer student and was offered the opportunity to grade-on to two journals. The grade-on criterion was that I needed to "book" a class; booking a class means you had the highest grade in that 1L course. Most schools do not allow this grade-on transfer to journals, however. This was a consideration for me, as the University of Florida, another law school that had offered me transfer admission, did not offer this option.

In the end, I chose the University of Florida and had to compete in the summer write-on competition. Because I didn't receive my transfer acceptance until late July, I joined the write-on competition late and had only a few days to write and finalize my case comment. In the end, I was offered admission to two journals, so while frustrating it was worth it.

CREDIT WHERE CREDIT IS DUE ... SOMETIMES

Most law schools will not accept all of your 1L credits. While the curricula for all ABA-accredited law schools are nearly identical, and while most first-year law school curricula have 30 credits, law schools nonetheless have widely varying policies on how many transfer credits they will accept. While one law school might accept 29 of 30 credits from your Original 1L School, another law school might accept only 19. As unbelievable as it might seem, we have even heard of a law school that will accept only six (6!) credits, nearly negating the entire first-year.

If your new New 2L School allows you to transfer with just one-half or two-thirds of your 1L credits, you will lose nearly a semester's worth of credits, work, and money. Correspondingly, if you forfeit credits when you transfer, you will be behind in housekeeping details as well as actual graduation: you might find yourself continuously being behind the eight ball registering for courses you want to take. As there are precious few options for some advanced courses, this is a consideration to make before accepting the transfer—and possibly a discussion with the New 2L School dean, if your case is reasonable and your interest sincere.

> In my first semester as a 2L transfer student, my initial experience was disappointing: as I was not accepted until the end of July, I had almost no class options for the fall semester. I essentially was forced to take whatever courses were available, simply because they were available. (And, as with most academic experiences, there's usually a reason some courses never seem to fill up.) Unfortunately for me, the good ones were closed, and the ones that weren't were of little interest.

While it's possible to plead your case to professors and deans, hoping they'll grant you at least one or two courses you'll actually enjoy taking, if you do transfer be prepared to deal with this. This can be especially problematic if transferring to a smaller law school, which tends to offer fewer (and smaller) elective courses.

Most schools hold early registration for the Fall semester at the end of the preceding spring. You will not have that option. Moreover, if you are lacking in credits relative to your new peers, you might find yourself in this position the following Spring semester, and possibly thereafter. In the often-exclusive world of registering for high-demand courses, this might be a serious detriment to enjoying your new experience.

> My New 2L School accepted 29 of my 30 credits. All the other 2L students had 30 credits. As grateful as I felt for having the opportunity to attend this new school, I did not realize how this single credit would affect my ability to register for classes. Because of my one-credit deficiency, I had to register for spring classes at the tail end of the other 2Ls, and again I missed out on courses I wanted to take because by the time I could register, my ideal classes were already closed.

Yet another hurdle that most transfer students do not take into consideration is that once you transfer, you have maxed out all your transfer, or off-campus, credits. Under the ABA guidelines, law schools require you to take at least two-thirds of your credits at your New 2L School. This means you cannot take any more classes away from your New 2L School. You may not study abroad, or take any transient classes elsewhere, or at least take them for credit towards your J.D. If you were hoping to take courses outside the law school—in another college within the research university affiliated with the prestigious law school, perhaps—you likely will not be able to do so.

It is *possible* for exceptions to be made, maybe. You'll need to be very persuasive with the law school's dean, meaning you'll need to have a clear and real reason for taking that class outside the law school, and it might involve creative scheduling for credit with a law professor's imprimatur or some cross-agreement among the university's colleges. Sometimes there are a few courses that are already jointly offered. It's worth checking if you're interested.

YET MORE TO CONSIDER

Aside from the academic hurdles, transferring law schools will be difficult emotionally and socially. Many students make their friends during their 1L year out of a shared experience—some might add shared traumatic experience. As a transfer student, you'll be on the outside of the social networking scene—and you'll certainly *feel* as if you're on the outside. Chances are you'll transfer with at least a few other transfer students—which can form the basis for a small social safety net, at least to start—but you will still feel left out.

If you transfer to a new school, especially in a different area of the state or country, be prepared for feeling a bit like you did if ever you changed schools as a kid. The experience can range from discomforting to terrifying, depending upon how quickly and easily you are at adjusting socially as well as academically. There are good people at your New 2L School, of course, so with a little effort you are likely to leave these worries behind within a month or so, if not sooner.

Here are a few ways to help meet and make new friends and future colleagues:

1. Do not attempt to answer every question a professor poses. You may have been the know-it-all at your old school, but for now, you are an outsider on somebody else's turf and you do not want to get labeled right off the bat as such. (In fact, even if you don't transfer, you really shouldn't try to be a know-it-all. Your future colleagues know a whole lot, too.)

2. Take a seat in the classroom where you feel most comfortable, but try not to sit on the end of a row as this will limit the number of people you will have a chance to interact with.

3. Go to your New 2L School's website and search the various clubs and organizations that are affiliated with the law school and the rest of the university. At your new school seek out the student organizations (student bar association, Thespians Lex, Law Students United for Ice Cream, you name it) and join the ones that interest you. On-campus organizations are always looking for new

members to help support their cause, and it will provide you with a way to meet people who share similar interests and concerns. Keep in mind, however, that 2L grades for a transfer student are still important.

4. Find out who else is a transfer student. Chances are the deans will have an orientation, get-together, or informal meeting, but if not, ask. Take the time and get to know them. Especially if you feel utterly alone at your new school, the bond that transfer students form with one another is similar to that shared among 1Ls. Also, other transfer students might have other friends at the law school or on campus, and they might be happy to open social doors for you.

A VIEW FROM THE INSIDE

Here are some thoughts from a dean of students at the University of Florida Levin College of Law on the many personal considerations in transferring:

Question: What is the number one question you receive from incoming transfer students, and how do you answer it?

Answer: The most frequently asked questions pertain to getting involved with organizations and meeting people, where to buy books, and where to live.

Question: If time permits, how early do you suggest an incoming transfer student arrive to get acclimated at their new law school?

Answer: This depends on the person. If a student is not familiar with the institution or town, they may want to arrive earlier than someone who has attended the institution for another degree program or who lived in the same town before. Generally, a student would want at least a week before classes begin to prepare for the upcoming semester such as buying books, organizing for class, extra-curricular activities, etc. Also, depending on whether or not the student is participating in OCI, the student may want to arrive even earlier. It simply depends on the student and his or her situation.

Question: What have you found to be the better resources in helping transfer students find a place to live?

Answer: I generally refer students to local apartment locators that do not charge a fee to assist them in finding a place to live. In addition, in the age of Facebook, students often post messages looking for roommates, places to live, etc. and this provides another resource that is becoming increasingly popular.

Question: How important do you feel attending the Transfer Orientation day is?

Answer: It is very important. Transferring students receive an overview of the new academic policies and procedures for which they are responsible. It is even more important as it provides an opportunity for the transfer students to meet with other students who are in the same situation, and these students also have an opportunity to meet members of the faculty and staff one-on-one and to ask questions in an open forum.

Question: What can you suggest to incoming transfer students to do before they arrive on campus?

Answer: From an administrative perspective, it is easier if a student takes care of the details that allow them to matriculate into the institution. Such details include ensuring official transcripts are sent to the Registrar's Office, immunization records are sent and received by the Student Health Care Center, and various other required details. This allows for less follow-up and alerting of students that they must take care of these details before they are allowed to register for classes and matriculate.

Question: What can incoming transfer students do to make your job easier?

Answer: A student can assist me in accomplishing what I need to do for them by following through with advice and instructions that I provide for them. Ultimately, this is making my job "easier" as the student is able to accomplish what he or she has set out to do, which typically results in fewer barriers to the student.

Question: One of the biggest transitions a transfer student has to make is the social one, what can you suggest transfer students to do in fostering new friendships and relationships with other students?

Answer: Whether a student is a transfer or not, to acclimate socially to a new and foreign environment a student should become involved with university and law school activities. There are numerous opportunities to become involved at the law school in addition to the main campus. These opportunities include student organizations, student government, intramural activities, and co-curricular activities. In addition, there are opportunities in the community that provide for interaction and meeting students off-campus.

Question: What do you feel is the #1 quality transfer students should possess to be successful at their new school?

Answer: Students should not be afraid to ask questions, whether it's an inquiry about academic policy, career advice, or simply getting involved in general. Also, success will depend on the student's goals while attending law school. Students are here for an education, and some will focus solely on this. However, if a student is looking for more than an education, then setting goals and implementing a plan to fulfill these goals is essential in being successful.

Kari A. Mattox is Assistant Dean of Students at the University of Florida Levin College of Law.

To Apply or Not To Apply: That Is The Question

We'll borrow the tiers conveniently provided by the ubiquitous *U.S. News* law school rankings. Tier 1 is comprised of law schools ranked 1-50; Tier 2 is comprised of law schools ranked from 51-100; Tier 3 and Tier 4 law schools are listed alphabetically.

At the top of Tier 1 are the Top 14, or the national law schools. One might parse the rest of Tier 1 (#15-50), and while there might be differences between, say, schools ranked between #15 and #20 as compared to those ranked between #45 and #50, for our purposes Tier 1 is comprised of the Top 14 and the remaining 36 law schools. This is in part because these tiers and sub-tiers are only approximate indicators, and, more importantly, because factors specific to you and your situation can and should become more important when the rankings are relatively close (*i.e.,* within a half-dozen to a dozen or so).

These *U.S. News* law school rankings have become the de facto standard for comparing law schools. Some try to avoid this, while others simply follow it without thinking about the other factors. You should take a middle road: these rankings are important—very important—but so too are your individual circumstances and wishes. Don't ignore either.

This section is to give you yet another balancing test, which we hope will be helpful as you decide which schools to apply to, and then which school to transfer to. The law school transfer process can sometimes seem quite arbitrary. Sometimes it is. We would love to present a chart and tell you that if you attend a T4 school and receive x class rank, then you will get into *y* law school. This, of course, is not how the transfer process works (or anything else, come to think of it). As with your 1L application, many factors are in play. As mentioned, our task is to help you through the transfer process, and to help you maximize your chances at your dream schools, and to help you through the actual transfer.

Much has been written about the *U.S. News* rankings, of course, and for our purposes we simply have to accept them as a given. Many transfer students are transferring for the rankings, expressly or implicitly, and for the impact that those rankings have on their job opportunities and status. We neither condemn nor applaud this, but it is important to understand that this is a common theme among transfer students (as it is among all law students), whether or not it is the primary stated goal.

In Chapter 4, we'll add to these scenarios a further analytical tool: that of considering five factors that each transfer applicant should consider. This is important in keeping these scenarios and discussions of rankings and tiers into perspective: these should not be all-or-nothing decisions.

Many factors are in play in the law school admission process, chief among them grades but certainly not only grades. A basic factor is whether the school you want to transfer to is transfer friendly. If it accepts just a handful of transfer students each year—and those reluctantly—chances are your chances are not great. If, however, the law school has chosen to take advantage of transfer applications, and dedicate admissions resources to this, as a matter of raw numbers that can have a big impact on your odds with that law school.

This book is written to help you maximize your chances before you transfer and opportunities when you transfer, but we of course cannot determine (or predict) your fate. Admissions deans and officers are, if anything, likely to be even more concerned in transfer applications with the subjective criteria that consume them with their 1L applications. Moreover, with transfers there is a greater chance to fine-tune the results of the prior year's acceptances and 1L class. If for whatever reason there's a demographic imbalance in the law school's student body, transfers are a magic way for a law school to restore that balance. Among these are the constellation of factors beyond your objective scores. (For 1Ls, that's LSAT and GPA; for transfers that's grades and then LSAT and GPA.) Among these factors are your class rank; Original 1L School's reputation; background (race, gender, age, as well as work experience, undergraduate education, home state, etc.); extra-curricular activities and extraordinary accomplishments that seem to have more resonance with law school grades under your belt; the number of 1Ls leaving the school you want to transfer to; and composition of 1Ls leaving. All are part of the admissions officers' concerns, and any one of these can have an impact—possibly a big impact—on your chances.

THE SCENARIOS

All law schools are not created equal. Here is one student's experience:

> I attended a T4 school that was provisionally accredited by the ABA. This meant I could sit for the bar and my law school would receive the same recognition as all other fully approved law schools until such time as the "provisional" part was deleted and it would be simply ABA-accredited. In all other respects, however, it was

the very bottom of the proverbial law school barrel. When I spoke with anyone at potential transfer schools, for example, some asked about my school because they had never heard of it, or they asked if it was accredited. These are not good questions to be asked. Those who had heard of it knew it was new, and almost visibly held their noses.

At the end of my 1L year I was ranked near the top of my class. Statistically, that left me with a good chance to break into the Tier 1 law schools. But that's far too simplistic a metric to use. One simply never knows the outcome. I did get admitted to a law school ranked around #23—a huge jump up from my T4 school—but was denied admission at another law school ranked around #85.

This book is designed to help you identify these various factors, both objective and especially subjective, and then use them to maximize your chances of sending out the best application you can so you can attend the best law school you can.

Scenario 1: You Attend a Tier 4 Law School. If you originally matriculated at a Tier 4 law school, transferring might be on your mind from the start. That written, for a T4 student it is even *more* important to know how and when to complete the transfer steps and how crucially important (and how) to keep your high grades and class rank.

Scenario 1 is the most aggressive, because the stakes are so high. A Tier 4 law school offers few career boosts, especially in a difficult job market. Thus, if you attend a Tier 4 law school, making the jump to a Tier 1 law school is almost a no brainer, if you can. While you may lose your grades, friends, and class rank, Tier 1 schools are well-established, have a large alumni base, and in the short, long, and medium run will be hugely beneficial for your career.

The waters become murkier when a Tier 4 student wants to transfer to a Tier 2 or especially a Tier 3 law school. Being more regional in nature (meaning job prospects tend to come from locales close to the law school's geographic area), a Tier 3 school has characteristics similar to those of a Tier 4 school, while a Tier 2 school is acutely aware of its status below Tier 1 and above Tiers 3 and 4 (because it's closer to T1 and because it wants to join the higher tier and distance itself from the lower ones). In such a case, it becomes more important to decide on personal issues, such as where you want to work upon graduation and the financial debt you are willing or able to incur. Unless you attend a Top 14 law school, it is vital to go to law school in the demographic area where you plan to practice. Outside of Top 14 (and, to a lesser degree, Tier 1) law schools, job prospects and potential offers usually come from employers in the same area as the law school.

If you go to a Tier 4 law school in California but want to practice in Florida, then transferring to a Tier 2 or 3 school in Florida makes good sense. If you attend a Tier 4 school in California, however, and want to stay and practice in California, transferring to a Tier 3 or even Tier 2 law school in Florida does not make sense. It will almost always be harder to get a job from far away if you do not attend a Top 14 (or, to a greater extent, Tier 1) law school. As for tuition, private tuition is not a primary concern if you attend a Top 14 law school; the financial gain is well worth the cost. When coming from a Tier 4 and transferring to a Tier 2 or Tier 3 law school, you should not discount the importance of tuition. Financial aid that you have to pay back—in other words, most of it—might seem amorphous when you sign for it. You never actually *see* the money, and you may not feel the weight of those multiple loans stacking up. When you are about to graduate and start searching for jobs, however, those loans and that mountainous debt will loom large. Think very, very seriously about private or out-of-state tuition costs before you even consider transferring.

I started at a Tier 4 law school. My LSAT was not outstanding and so I accepted a Tier 4 invitation in my home state, with in-state tuition. While LSAT scores alone are not conclusive as to how well one will perform in law school, I attended the first day and knew I wanted to transfer out.

This is a dangerous game. The cardinal rule is *never go to a law school you would not mind graduating from, with its name on your diploma for the rest of your life.* Statistically, this makes sense. If your 1L class has 200 students in it, only 10 students can be in the top 5%; which is usually the crucial percentage to be in if you want even a shot to make the glamorous Tier 4 to Tier 1 transfer jump. Odds are, you won't be in the top 5%; you might just be with the other 95% of the class. You just never know. So despite the cardinal rule, I figured that someone has to be in the top 5%, so why not me?

Being in the top 5% will be difficult. Very difficult. But it is also very doable with hard work and a focused approach. After my 1L year I was in the top 2% of my 1L class. After many, many transfer applications (and about $3,000), I finally started getting admissions decisions, and was accepted to a school ranked in the middle of Tier 1. The school was outside the area where I wanted to practice, and I would have to pay out-of-state tuition. I was also accepted to the top-ranked law school in my state—ranked around 40-50, so technically in Tier 1—and I decided in the end to attend that law school.

This was a hard choice to make but it came down to logistics. I did not get into a Top 14 school. I was waitlisted at one (Georgetown), but was ultimately rejected. If you don't crack the Top 14 law schools, location needs to play a *big* role in your decision, along with tuition. In my example, the out-of-state tuition was $35,000 per year, while in-state tuition was around $10,000. Without living expenses (which would have been higher at the far-away school), that was a $60,000 difference in tuition for the next two years. Further, the out-of-state school was located in an expensive downtown city where a one-bedroom apartment cost $2,000 per month—or another $48,000 on top of the $60,000 tuition differential. Consider the city as well when you decide to transfer.

Scenario 2 – You Attend a Tier 2 or Tier 3 Law School. There are two schools of thought here. If you are in the top 5% of your Tier 2 or Tier 3 1L class, and transferring into a Top 14 is a real possibility, you might just want to go for it. The Top 14 schools are national schools and the most prestigious law schools in the country. They will get you a job, and keep getting you jobs.

What if you are not top 5%? As hard as this is, you might want to consider staying at your Tier 2 or Tier 3 law school. If you have solid grades to potentially transfer up (but not to a Top 14 school), this also means you have a high class rank and potential law review or journal invitee offers. While it might be beneficial to throw out a few long-shot transfer applications to transfer-friendly Top 14 law schools, moving from a Tier 2 or Tier 3 law school to a lower ranked Tier 1 law school might not be worth the trouble, hassle, and losses, especially if the lower-ranked Tier 1 law school is not in the same area in which you want to practice. An exception might be from a Tier 3 to a Tier 1 law school, if it otherwise is a school you would be delighted to attend. A second exception might occur if your state has a Tier 1 public law school, which if admitted would give you in-state tuition and clear advantages. Ultimately this is a gut-reaction Question: do you really, truly want to undergo all of the challenges we mention, and will it be worth it, emotionally and financially?

In favor of staying put, ranking in the top 5-10% in the class of a Tier 2 or Tier 3 law school that's in the area where you want to practice will almost certainly be sufficient to do well in a law career. You keep your high grades, class rank, and law review invitation. In short, don't transfer to a Tier 1 law school just because you can, and certainly not just because you think you're supposed to. Transfer to a Tier 1 school only if it *is* just too good to pass up: if it's a Tier 1 school you really like and it's in the area where you want to practice, or if it's a Top 14 law school. Even so, don't ignore the very real costs you will undertake for a new school.

Scenario 3: You're at T1 School and Want to Transfer Up to T14. Let's assume for the moment that you're at a T1 law school. You probably did rather well in undergrad and likewise did well on your LSAT. While top grades at a T1 school can be a ticket to a Big Law job—especially in that locale—there *is* a difference between T1 and T14. Let's further assume that you want to crack into the T14 national law schools because of the prestige (and the sweater vest and country club membership that seem packaged with the T14 diploma). With your heart set on the T14 club, here is your balancing test: if you like your T1 law school, will grade-on to law review, and will receive a generous scholarship for staying (always good to ask!), those all strongly favor staying put.

The two key elements are your T1 future-in-hand and your T14 dreams. If your T1 law school is in the area where you want to practice law after graduation, then it might be a no-brainer to stay. You will keep your high class rank, grade-on to law review, probably receive a sizeable academic scholarship, and have a good shot at a top job via OCI. It's hard to walk away from that.

What if your T1 law school is not in the area in which you want to practice? Or, what if your T1 law school is in the area you want to practice, but there is also a higher-ranked T14 school in the same area? As one example, if you attend Fordham, in New York City, but want to attend Columbia or NYU—and have a good shot—there are compelling reasons to make the switch. Columbia and NYU both carry more weight, in New York and across the country. Ten years from now no one will ask you what your GPA or class rank was. The only question will be: "Where did you go to law school?" That is, to be sure, a strong reason to make the switch.

Or, what if you have absolutely no idea where you want to live? Or, what if you simply want to attend a T14 school? The waters become murky as you start down the path of transferring. T1 law schools are great law schools; T14 law schools are national law schools. The key to this question might well boil down to a highly subjective test: are you willing to give up all of the above in exchange for that T14 diploma (and vest and country club membership)? If so, this is a good problem: it's hardly a "mistake" to transfer to a T14 law school. But, even so, you will still need to prepare for the logistical and personal obstacles in the transfer itself, just as with all other transfer students. Thus, even if you're in the enviable position of transferring from a T1 to a T14 law school, you will still need to pay attention to the many challenges we describe in this book.

Scenario 4: You Want to Make a Lateral Move or Even Transfer Down.
Scenario 3 might be called the personal move: the transfer happens because of personal motives outside of academics. Academically, unless you want to transfer to a similarly-ranked law school that is nationally known for a certain type of law you want to practice, a lateral or down transfer does not make sense. A handful of Tier 3 or Tier 4 schools might be known for a specialized type of law (often because of a single professor or small group of professors), so that may be a reason for a lateral or downward transfer in the rankings— but it's not likely. Keep in mind what you will lose: your grades, class rank, law review, friends, money. Again, unless you transfer to that new school for a highly special reason, this type of transfer is based

on personal motives, such as family. This is not wrong, and if important to you, that might well be your answer. But it is crucially important to understand your motives before you set this transfer train in motion.

Scenario 5: Part-Time to Full-Time, or Vice Versa. This is a fairly limited issue, but it occurs frequently enough that it might be a concern for you. If you are a part-time law student seeking to transfer to a different law school, you'll run into an additional concern besides the one about which tier each school is in. Most law schools require a certain number of credits to be eligible to transfer. If you attend your Original 1L School part-time and have 15 to 18 credits at the end of your 1L "year," most schools will not allow you to apply for transfer status until you accrue more credits. As you're on a 4-year graduation track, for most part-time students, this means continuing in their second year at the Original 1L School and then applying to transfer when you have accrued the required 30 or so credits.

Conversely, if you are a 1L who goes to school full time, you might want to consider applying to a part-time program if your grades are not at the top of the class and you still want to transfer, or if you want to take a shot at a higher-ranked school that offers a part-time program. As can be seen on the Law School Admission Council website, the average GPA and LSAT score for part-time students is lower than it is for full time students. Additionally, schools tend to be more lenient with part-time seats in a class. That written, it can be beneficial to apply to a part-time program when you transfer to advance your chances for admission. Further, some schools such as Georgetown, George Washington, and Stetson University allow you to apply to both programs. While you do have to pay double application fees in some schools, you have at least in theory an increased of chance of admittance to one of their programs.

TO TRANSFER OR NOT TO TRANSFER

Pros	Cons
Increased reputation of law school and pedigree.	Loss of class rank and 1L grades; loss of law review grade-on invitation.
Increased alumni base; increased networking opportunities.	Higher private or out-of-state tuition (if applicable).
Better OCI and initial job opportunities, increased salaries, and better long-term career outlook.	New school, new city, and new peers and professors; potential loss of 1L school relationship with peers and professors; stress of the unknown; stress of comparing yourself to new students.
Increased clerkship opportunities.	Loss of scholarships; transfers rarely, if ever, are offered scholarships to transfer; many scholarships do not apply to transfer students until after they complete their first semester.
Increased intellectual challenge; more research opportunities and often better facilities.	Have to write onto journal (grades don't transfer).
Higher-ranked school tend to run a higher grade curve.	May lose credits. If so, behind the rest of the class in registering for classes.
Move to a preferred job market.	Cannot take classes "off campus" (*i.e.,* no study abroad or transient credits).

FREQUENTLY ASKED QUESTIONS

What are the *U.S. News* law school rankings?

A report put together every year that ranks all the ABA-accredited law schools in the country. Factors considered in the rankings include objective as well as subjective criteria, self-reported, such as LSAT and GPA scores of admitted students, reputational rank according to professors and practitioners, job placement success, bar passage rate, faculty and student data, and the law library.

When will I hear back from the transfer schools?

The law school transfer process has a short turnaround time. Once your application materials are complete (*i.e.*, all materials the admissions committee requires have been received), the admissions decision is usually made in one to six weeks. Some schools send out their acceptances in midsummer, while some do not send out acceptances until early August—giving you only a week or so to pick up and move.

How does the Admissions Committee inform students of their transfer admission decision?

It varies, but given the time constraints schools use the telephone or email to inform you of an acceptance, with a letter to follow. Traditionally, a snail-mail letter is a sign of rejection or waitlist.

How should I go about looking for housing?

Talk with the admissions department or student affairs at your New 2L School. Some schools have housing designated for law students. Most will try to help a transfer student with information on available housing. Also check craigslist.org and local internet sites. (But be careful, of course.)

How long do I have to accept the transfer offer?

Like much else in the transfer process, things happen quickly. When you are notified that you are accepted, you will usually be given anywhere from two weeks to a month to make your decision. Most schools offer around a two-week timeframe and then see how many transfer students have accepted their offers. At that point, they can send out additional offers to waitlisted students. As with your 1L application, if you know you aren't going to attend, build good karma by letting the law school know when you do, thus giving the waitlisted soul an extra week or so to pack, rejoice, and prepare.

When should I fill out my FAFSA and which schools should I put down?

Fill out your FAFSA just as you would for your Original 1L School. However, be sure to add your potential New 2L Schools on the list of schools to receive your FAFSA report.

A VIEW FROM THE LAW SCHOOL

Here is an interview with the dean of admissions from one of the top U.S. law schools, the University of Virginia School of Law:

Question: What factors are given the most attention when reviewing a transfer application?

Answer: Without a doubt, the most important factor is your law school performance. We do not look at your LSAT or undergraduate GPA very much. In the direct admissions process, we use an applicant's LSAT and GPA to predict how well we think they will do in law school. In the transfer process, we know how well they did.

Question: Is the review process of transfer applications any different than the review process an admissions office goes through for incoming 1L applications?

Answer: We get decisions out to applicants much more quickly in the transfer process so that they can fully participate in our on-grounds interview process.

Question: Are transfer applications decided by a single Dean or a transfer committee?

Answer: I review the transfer applications by myself, which hastens the decision making process. This is important for the reason stated above.

Question: When reviewing a transfer application is there a "sliding scale" with regard to the grades a student receives in relation to where the student received those grades? If so, how much does where a potential transfer student receive his or her grades matter?

Answer: To some extent yes. Most of our successful transfer applicants are in the top 10-15% of their class, but due consideration is given to the relative competitiveness of the sending school. We take transfer applicants from peer schools from somewhat deeper in the class.

Question: Besides the required materials (letters of recommendation, transfer statement, résumé) do you suggest transfer applicants include a writing sample? If so, should it be their entire appellate brief or the argument section extrapolated?

Answer: Transfer students need not submit any additional material. They are free to do so, but we do not require it.

Question: To facilitate the transfer process, do you prefer electronic or paper documents when sending the required materials to a school?

Answer: We require an electronic application and LSDAS report sent to us directly from LSAC. But the letter of recommendation from the law school professor may be sent directly to us.

Question: How much of a benefit do you see transfer students attaining with regard to OCI?

Answer: We reserve spots for transfer students in our on-grounds interview process. Our Assistant Dean for Career Services, Polly Lawson, is a 2001 graduate of the Law School (and my classmate) and was a transfer student here. She is particularly attuned to the needs of the transfer students.

Question: What are some benefits transfer students bring to your school?

Answer: It is always nice to bring in students with different experiences, and transfer students have the benefit of seeing how things run at a different law school. I like to think they bring the very best of what they learned there to Virginia.

Question: Why do you think some law schools are reluctant to admit larger transfer classes?

Answer: I am not sure. Twenty transfer students is just about right for us.

Question: How does race, gender, and ethnicity play a role in being admitted as a transfer student? Is it the same evaluation as to incoming 1L applications?

Answer: There is no difference in the transfer pool. Race, gender, and ethnicity are among the diversity factors UVA takes into consideration, such as undergraduate majors and prior work experience. UVA places a lot of emphasis on geographic diversity.

Question: With the current state of the economy, do you feel the numbers and competition regarding transfer students will increase? If so, why?

Answer: We experienced a 20% increase in the number of direct applications this year. We now have approximately 7,900 applications for the 350 spots in the first-year class. I expect an increase in transfer applications this year because I think students will be looking to maximize their career prospects in this tough economy. But I do not think it will be up 20%. Then again, I did not expect our direct pool to be up by that much either.

Question: If you had to convey one message to potential transfer students regarding the transfer process, what would it be?

Answer: Study hard. Your law school performance is paramount in our transfer process.

Jason Wu Trujillo is Senior Assistant Dean for Admissions and Financial Aid at the University of Virginia School of Law.

3

THE TRANSFER APPLICATION

Though similar in many respects to the first-year application process, applying to law school as a transfer student brings its unique challenges. From the mad rush of getting your transcripts, letters of recommendation, and myriad application documents in order (and actually "in"), the transfer application is its own kind of beast. As before, you only have one shot. Like a rollercoaster, it has its highs, its lows, and very highs and very lows. But, as with all rides, there is an end.

As daunting as it sounds to tackle the whole law school application process again—and with the mad rush of first year, no less—the actual application itself is the most familiar part of the transfer process. Why? Well, you are filling out the same application as you did as a 1L. The difference is that instead of checking the first-year box you check the transfer box. Further, the law schools using the LSAC (*i.e.,* all of them you would want to apply to) already have most of your information they'll need.

One note in the actual transfer application: If the law school you are applying to offers a part-time program, consider checking both boxes. By checking both boxes, you might give yourself a greater opportunity to gain acceptance to the school. If you believe the part-time program is not for you, you might still consider it, as you might be able to leap-frog your way into the full-time program with a stellar performance and good behavior at your new school. This option should be discussed with the Student Affairs Office at your school.

The application fee will most likely be the same fee that 1Ls pay. Be sure to confirm whether the fee is paid online or the school requires a physical check.

WAIVING THE APPLICATION FEE

Don't be afraid to ask a school for a fee waiver, if appropriate. This request is simple and can be done through email. In the email include whatever forms the office requires plus a brief statement on why you are requesting that the application fee to be waived and attach a copy of your résumé. Attaching your résumé does not harm you as it: (1) introduces you to the Admissions Office before you apply; (2) allows the Admissions Office to view your past accomplishments; and (3) expresses your intention to transfer to that school. It won't likely have a major impact, but every little bit helps.

Below is a sample email requesting a law school waive the application fee:

Dear Admissions Committee,

My name is _____. I recently completed my first year of law school at ____(Original 1L School)____ in ____(City)____. I am interested in applying to transfer to your law school, and I wanted to inquire about an application fee waiver. Enclosed please find the requisite financial information.

My stats include a ____(Law school GPA)____ from my first year in law school placing me ____(rank)____ out of ____(rest of class)___, and ____(Undergraduate GPA)____ from the ____(Undergrad School)____, and ____(any extracurricular activities you find important)____.

Attached is a copy of my résumé. I look forward to hearing from you.

Thank You,

___(Your Name)____

At the end of the day, with multiple applications going out, your application fees can easily add up to hundreds of dollars. If you are fortunate enough to obtain an application fee waiver, your application will only cost you $12 for the LSAC request to send your material to the school and whichever postage you choose to use when sending your Letter of Good Standing. In the end, to borrow the old expression, "It doesn't hurt to ask; the worst thing they can say is 'No.'" With application fees ranging from $20-$100 and pizza money running low (or car insurance bills coming due), this could be the easiest money you save. It's worth a shot, right?

EARLY ACTION

Early Action is an admissions process that a limited number of law schools offer for transfer students. Importantly, the law schools that promote early action include some of the top schools in the country: University of Chicago (#7), Georgetown (#14), Washington University in St. Louis (#19), and Boston College (#26). Early Action encompasses all of the same steps in the normal transfer admissions process, with the difference being that you have only your Fall semester grades to take into account. The Early Action programs at these schools tend to start accepting applications for Admission for the following Fall semester in the beginning of February, and the application deadline is usually mid-to-late March.

The beauty of Early Action is that your acceptance, deferral, or denial will come prior to you taking your Spring exams; therefore, you will know if you were able to make the jump before you sit down to go through exams again. Before you get too excited, this does not mean that you can just completely bomb your 1L Spring semester exams and expect to walk into the doors of one of the nation's best law schools. The process is similar to the one you might have had in your senior year in high school, where you find out what colleges you have been admitted to before your finals—before "Senioritis"—but they *still* demanded your final high school transcripts. It works the same way if you are fortunate enough to gain acceptance to one of these law schools through Early Action.

For those of you who are not so fortunate to get a "golden ticket" through early admissions, we shall discuss what the other two responses indicate. Deferral indicates that you are still being considered. This should motivate you more than ever to ace your spring exams. Here the school is saying, "We like your application, but just need a little bit more to make an honest assessment as to your performance." Obviously, you were hoping, maybe even praying, for an early acceptance, as that would take a load off your mind and bring your stress levels down, but getting deferred should only drive you to push yourself all the more: your goal is within reach.

Denial is definitely not the letter you were looking to receive. The only positive, perhaps, is that you can stop worrying. Now you know where to target your other applications. It might be that the leap is simply too great, and maybe some other law schools you're interested in will be interested in you. Sometimes an even higher-ranked law school might be interested in you! Early Action is a highly competitive process. Keep that in mind. Not getting an early admission does not eliminate you from contention for regular admissions or for admission to other law schools you might consider transferring to.

REGULAR ADMISSIONS

Most law schools do not have an Early Action Program; you thus apply through their regular admissions process, which typically begins between May 15th and July 1st. Within this timeframe, each school will have a different date when you can start sending the application materials to them. As the turnaround time for regular admissions is short, we *strongly* encourage you to begin filling out your applications once exams are over and, as soon as possible, send in your application(s), letters of recommendation, Transfer Statement(s), and any other documents you believe to be pertinent. By doing this early, the school will start a file on you as the school awaits the rest of your application so it can be deemed complete. As with your 1L process, your application is considered "Complete" only when *all* of your materials are received. Most likely, the last document you will be sending is your Letter of Academic Standing.

Be sure to confirm the application deadline and when each school wants your application complete; there is a big difference between the two. The application deadline is the deadline for your application and application fee. Think of it as you indicating your interest versus the Complete deadline, when all required documents must be received. Law schools understand that the transfer process does not involve a lot of time, and they know it may take you some time to procure letters of recommendation and to get your Transfer Statement. Thus, most law schools have the application deadline preceding the Complete deadline (so they know how many transfer applications they will have), and leaving them sufficient time from the Complete deadline to decide and then notify the transfer applicants of their fate before the next semester begins. As future lawyers, you need to engage in your own due diligence and confirm the deadlines for each law school to which you are applying.

WAITLISTED

Similar to the Early Action Program, as an applicant you can be accepted or denied; instead of a deferred decision until your spring grades are released, however, you can be waitlisted. A law school will include waitlist applicants for a number of reasons, mostly involving its own internal needs. Law schools are well aware that applicants apply to multiple schools. Therefore, if a student accepts an offer to attend one school and thus declines an offer from another school, the school that was declined can now offer admittance to another applicant. (This can depend upon that school's assumptions of how many from its pool of accepted applicants will in turn accept the offer. This, of course, leads to applicant nail-biting at the end of the admissions season.)

As a courtesy to other transfer students, if you are in the fortunate position to receive multiple offers from schools, you should decline as quickly as possible if you know that you will not be attending that school. By declining as early as possible, you give other applicants a chance of being admitted to a school *they* desire to attend, and give them a little more time to get ready.

LETTERS OF RECOMMENDATION

Believe it or not, the transfer application process—whether you are going into your first semester of law school with the intention to transfer or not—begins on the first day of class. From Day 1 you are dealing with a host of new faces, opinions, policies, procedures, thoughts, philosophies, personalities, and ideologies. From where you sit to how you conduct yourself the first time you are called upon to discuss a case in class, the critics are out, and these critics will help to shape, mold, and piece together your "once in a lifetime" law school experience. These critics play a vital role in shaping the everyday decisions that you may take for granted, as someone is always watching, and come transfer application time you may need to rely on one of these critics for help. Not only do the critics sit amongst you in class, they also conduct the class.

When attempting to transfer law schools, the school you are wishing to attend will require at least one letter of recommendation from a law professor. Depending on the requirements of the schools you are wishing to gain acceptance to, some may require two or three letters of recommendation from your law professors. The main reason a law school wants to read letters from your professors is so they can gain insight to your performance and demeanor inside the classroom. Yes, your grades are indicative how well you can perform on an exam, but the letters of recommendation provides the law school with insight from your professor on something far less tangible: how you react, think, and behave.

Before approaching your professor, take a step back and ask yourself, "If I were in the professor's shoes, could I write a letter detailing: (1) excellent performance in the classroom; (2) an ability to articulate thoughts and ideas coherently; (3) good participation; and (4) an ability to raise complex questions and alternate arguments not mentioned in the case." If you hesitate before answering in the affirmative, you have more work to do.

When approaching a professor for a letter to transfer law schools, do some *serious* research on your professor. Do not simply walk up after class one day and saying, "Hey, Professor X, can you write me a letter of recommendation so I can transfer law schools?" To you it might not seem like a big deal, but asking for a letter of recommendation to transfer law schools is not like asking for a letter of recommendation from a college professor to get into law school as a 1L.

First, if you have not already done so, review your professor's bio on your school's webpage. For the most part, the bio will include the professor's undergraduate and graduate schools, law school, and often honors (*cum laude, magna cum laude,* and *summa cum laude*). Next, it will include the classes they teach and past institutions at which they have taught, including how long they taught there. The bio will include professional accomplishments, cases, publications, and professional activities. You will get a sense of your professor's interests, and more importantly see whether your professor attended or taught at one of the law schools you are attempting to transfer into. Also, it provides a way for you to become more knowledgeable about and personal with a professor as you may be able to strike up a conversation dealing with a mutual connection or interest.

For example, your torts professor has published articles in the area of environmental law and you had no idea of it until reading their bio. You might approach the professor in this manner, "Professor _____, I noticed that you have published extensively in the area of Littoral Environmental Law."

[Note: your research should be more detailed than merely a catchphrase like "environmental law," which nearly everyone professes to know. We made up "littoral environmental law," but the point is that your question should show that you're not just "going through the motions" to get what you want.]

After a few minutes' discussion of the professor's interests, casually mention, "I have been fortunate enough to do well academically, ranking *x* out of *xxx,* and I have an interest in practicing in this area. The opportunities don't seem as plentiful as they are at ABC School of Law, however, and I am considering applying to transfer there. What are your thoughts?"

Notice what's happening. Rather than a single statement—a "Gimme"—this should really be a series of conversations. We tend to babble on about ourselves when we should be focusing on building a genuine relationship. Try to avoid a "me, me, me" focus, and instead focus on the actual substance of what it is you're discussing. Importantly, this discussion should begin earlier than the time you actually need the letter.

What you seek to do is to show a mutual interest (assuming there is one), show your initiative and qualities, and ask for advice. The last point is crucial. Your professors have been around for a long while, with knowledge, contacts, and advice that is valuable. It's important that you approach them with respect and care, and take advantage—in a good way—of them and the ways in which they can help.

If, on the other hand, you learn that your professor has attended or has previously taught at a law school you are interested in transferring to, you might approach your Professor in this manner, "Professor Y, I understand you attended/taught at XYZ School of Law. I am very interested in attempting to transfer to XYZ because [list your reasons ... your *good* reasons]. If you don't mind, I was hoping you could share with me some of your insight and experiences there."

If the professor has good things to say and after you have developed a rapport, then when the topic suggests itself you ask about the letter of recommendation as you hope to have just as great of an experience at that school.

Chances are your professor—who knows what's what—will know exactly what you need and where you're going (both figuratively and literally). For that reason especially, it's important to be genuine and not to be "letter greedy." If you're just after a piece of paper, you'll likely get one. It won't, however, be one to help you get an answer from the admissions office you want to read if you're treating it as merely a pro forma obligation. Accept that this is among the most highly subjective parts of the transfer application process—if not *the* most highly subjective part. It's up to you to meet that challenge.

As part of this, you should be able to articulate exactly why you believe transferring law schools is in your best interest. You should write down your reasons so that *you* know the reasons why. This should not be forced, and should be part of an extended conversation, as with the woman who built relationships with professors and successfully transferred to Harvard Law School. That might or might not have been the deciding factor ... but if we had to guess, that's the way we'd bet.

Also, be prepared to discuss what you'll be giving up. Again, this is as much to make sure that you actually know the answers as much as for the professor—but it's still important for both.

Be prepared as well to respond to your professor's questions:

1. Why will transferring help you?

2. Why will your new school help you achieve what you want to achieve in practicing law?

3. Are there any potential incentives your current school could provide you to reconsider transferring schools? [Hint: scholarships.]

4. If you've mentioned multiple schools, do you have a preference of one school over another? Why?

5. Have you discussed the idea of transferring with any other professors?

Be prepared to answer these and any other questions your professor might throw your way. Even if you earned an "A" in their class, some professors might hesitate to write a letter for you. This hesitance can come from a sense of loyalty to their law school, animosity towards (or ignorance of) the transfer process in general, a sense that you will not be able to succeed at the school you are trying to transfer to, or any number of personal reasons.

Once a professor agrees, you should provide them with a copy of your unofficial transcript, a copy of your résumé, a personal narrative that lists your accomplishments and qualities beyond those listed in your résumé, and a completed LSAC consent form (which is the same form that you used for your 1L application into law school). When done, if a copy is given to you, be sure to make a copy for your records. If your professor gives the original to you instead, you should submit the letter directly to the school via mail and, if a copy is available, to the LSAC via mail or fax. Be sure to check with the schools that you are transferring to on how they would prefer to receive them, as some prefer not to use the LSAC for transfer applications. If you plan on sending the letter to the LSAC, the quickest way for LSAC to process the letter is via fax. Be sure to remember to mail or fax *both* the consent form and the letter together to prevent any unnecessary delays, as well as make a copy for your own records.

A point that might not occur to those who assume that résumés are all-purpose devices that relieve the creator of further obligation. Your purpose is to help your professor write an *excellent* recommendation. The résumé alone is not sufficient for that purpose. It is useful, however, to remind them of your qualities and to highlight additional facts that might not have come out in your conversations. That is the real task: you should have a sufficiently engaged relationship with whomever you're asking to write on your behalf that they don't really need to see a résumé to write a letter for you. The résumé is the side show. The main event is the hour you've spent here and there discussing whatever points of law and philosophy you find mutually interesting.

Asking for a letter of reference "blind"—from professors who probably know you about as well as they know their grocery clerk—is just asking for a bad letter. It's far better to focus on those professors with whom you have a genuine rapport.

LETTERS FROM OTHERS

Law schools are most concerned (almost *solely* concerned) with letters from your 1L professors, who are in the best position to attest to your law school performance, aptitude, and qualities. Letters from others who know you can play an influential factor in your transfer application: past professors, past coaches, a judge you worked for, a senior partner at a law firm you've worked in part-time, or distinguished alumni from the school you hope to transfer into. If you choose to include a letter from someone else other than a professor from your first-year law classes, the letter should demonstrate why that person is the writer, and a professional relationship between you and the author. It should also be crystal clear, implicitly, why that person is the *best* person to speak to your qualities.

A letter focusing on your personal qualities should have sufficient indication of your professional qualities as well. Its author should be able to speak candidly about your ability to succeed at a new law school and why they believe you would be a uniquely good addition to their law school. Their ability to mention specific instances where you rose to the challenge, or overcame adversity (detailing with some specificity why that law school cannot go wrong with admitting you) is crucial to an admissions committee giving such a letter any weight. In many cases, it's the "tipping point" in your favor (or against) for a highly subjective evaluation of competitor-applicants who are equally superbly qualified. After all, if nearly everyone who applies is at or near the top of their first-year class, what is going to distinguish you in the eyes of the admissions committee?

For example, if your dad knows a hot-shot senior partner at a big time law firm—yet you have never worked for him before—a boilerplate letter from that senior partner will not fly. Just because the letterhead is coming from someone at a Vault 5 firm will *not* impress the dean. This will not help your cause, and might actually impede it. Such "name dropping" is not going to help your chances, as such a letter does not provide the admissions committee with an inside look at your qualifications, abilities, and character. A sincere letter from an attorney at a smaller firm for whom you've worked since college will be infinitely better.

Moreover, if you include any such letter, you *must* still include at least one letter from a first-year law professor.

DETAILS

For an application involving Early Action, you should mail the letter of recommendation directly to the school. To borrow the legal phrase, time is of the essence. For regular applications, you can simply send it to LSAC with the rest of the application (make sure your school takes transfer applications through LSAC, otherwise you will have to send them on your own). Once in LSAC, it is the same process as if you were applying as a 1L. You just click on the letters that you want sent to a specific school and submit the application.

A thank you letter to the professor(s) who wrote you letters is an absolute must. It is preferably hand-written (if your penmanship isn't awful). This demonstrates a sincere gesture of appreciation and a civility that will be noted. Such a habit goes a long way in helping to develop, foster, and maintain positive relationships with others in the legal world, and in life as well. It is also a sincere recognition for the time that your professor is devoting to *your* cause. After all, your professor has other things to do—including worry about their own research and work—and writing letters of recommendations isn't among the most thrilling of those tasks.

You should, as well, do this now. Not tomorrow. Not next week. *Now*. What is left for "later" is invariably shuffled lower on your list of priorities, and then forgotten. Before you know it you'll be embarrassed to send anything as its tardiness will merely highlight your lack of attention and care. You never know when you'll need to ask for the next letter, and the whole point of building a relationship is not to ask for something only when it's obvious that it's "all about me." Break this habit, now.

Send the thank you letter, now.

TRANSFER STATEMENT

Your grades and the law school where you earned those grades play the lead role in determining your acceptance or denial to a new school. Letters of recommendation, along with the Transfer

Statement, can tip the scale. They can be (and often are) the critical difference for the borderline *maybe*.

For some, the Transfer Statement might be just a formality. For most, it is anything but. It is absolutely essential, and could be the essay that changes the rest of your life.

PERSONAL VERSUS TRANSFER STATEMENTS

Attempting to sit down and write an essay about yourself is probably one of the most frustrating parts of any application, college, 1L, or transfer. Before you begin you start asking yourself a series of questions, and even when you're onto something good you start to doubt whether you really are. From the simple to the ethereal, these nagging doubts keep coming:

What should I write about?

Can I use the same Personal Statement from my 1L application? Should I?

Do I really have an interesting story to tell?

Does it really *have* to be that many words?

Why can't I write it that way?

Should I really tell them about *that?*

Do I tell the truth about my reasons for transferring? What *are* the best reasons to transfer?

Do I talk about my 1L school? What do I say?

Okay. Let's first discuss the similarities between the 1L Personal Statement and the 2L Transfer Statement:

Length. Your Transfer Statement should be of similar length to your Personal Statement. Often it is expressly limited to a specific page or word count. If so, you must meet that requirement *exactly*. (Usually these are maximum limitations. If so, you can be slightly under, but you cannot be over, even by one word.)

Ideally you should be able to introduce yourself and why you want to transfer to that particular school in two pages. Three at the absolute max. For the same reasons, when applying to school as a potential 2L, a concise Transfer Statement should offer a snapshot of your goals and motives for applying to that particular school. Some schools, such as UC–Berkeley (Boalt Hall), will receive 200-250 transfer applications. It is simply not feasible for them to read 4-5 page essays from each applicant. Moreover, their assumption is that if you cannot figure out how to convey a simple theme in a 2-3 page essay, that's an easy answer right there. As much as you are pressed for time, the admissions office is juggling the same issues, times two hundred.

The essay gives the law school an opportunity to preview your writing ability, both technical and stylistic. Can you write, and can you *write?* Much like your appellate brief, every word counts, and the Transfer Statement allows a committee to see if you can get straight to the point, persuasively, without losing the reader's interest. Convincing the reader to choose you over someone else is a tall order—and that's why this is such an important component.

Content. Writing about oneself may be one of the most difficult tasks, but as with the 1L Personal Statement, distinguishing yourself from the rest of the field is the single-most important aspect of the Transfer Statement. You want to stand out—in a good way. How can you, in two pages, make someone remember who you are over everyone else? At least this time around it's a little easier to stand out as the number of transfer applications is far smaller than for incoming 1Ls. For the most part, everyone applying is going to meet the threshold needed to qualify on grades. You must therefore ask yourself, "What unique quality do I possess is going to make a total stranger believe in me?"

Determining that quality—or some event in your life—to differentiate yourself from other applicants is almost the easy part. Tying in reasons of leaving one school to pursue your goals by attending another school is the harder part. The ability to intertwine and connect your reasons for wanting to transfer to a particular school along with your unique experience(s) is extremely challenging. More on this in the Difference section.

Tone. The first-person approach many of us take in writing the Personal Statement does not differ when writing your Transfer Statement.

THE DIFFERENCE A YEAR MAKES

The most notable difference in drafting your Transfer Statement involves its content. As you mull your Transfer Statement over and over with countless revisions, edits, and second-guessing to see if you have provided the reader with the best snapshot of yourself, it is hard not to obsess over this 500-word document that could change your life. Unlike the Personal Statement, the Transfer Statement asks you to go one step further in not only identifying a character trait, experience, or adversity that you have encountered or overcome that makes you distinct from the rest of the field, but you must now incorporate specific reasons of why you want to go to that specific law school. This format is not as open a process as your 1L application was. The key to writing an effective Transfer Statement is being able to intertwine why or how you are "special" with the specific reasons why you want—need—to transfer to their law school.

Let's first go over a list of specific reasons you can offer:

1. A desire to practice in the region where the New 2L School is located, and the reasons why. For example, wanting to transfer to a school in Miami for a passion to practice immigration law, or wanting to transfer to a school in New York City for a passion to practice in corporate litigation.

2. An interest in a specific program the transfer law school specializes in. For example, an interest in attending *x* law school because of its nationally recognized environmental law program, or an interest in attending *y* law school because of their strong presence in trial advocacy.

3. Comparing your interest in a program or clinic that is available at the transfer school, but your current school does not offer, and why this program or clinic appeals directly to you and the direction that you want to take in your career.

4. Intentions to contribute to scholarly research (usually with some track record in research, such as with a graduate degree).

5. How you believe attending the transfer school will help you accomplish your career goals.

6. Personal reasons, such as needing to be closer to home to play a large role in a sibling's life, or a change in job for a spouse or fiancée.

The above can all be good reasons to tailor your Transfer Statement to a particular school. Focus on one or two of them and attempt to tie them in with your story that will set you apart from the rest of the field.

Each of these examples assumes that you have some concrete way to tie your interest into what you've already done. It's dangerous to talk about an "interest" in, say, environmental law if you've never done anything other than go camping as a kid. If it's to further your master's degree in forestry, then you're much more likely to find success with that line of argument. Likewise, talking about wanting to be in corporate litigation will be suspicious if you've never done anything involving finance. Sure, it's possible that this is why you're in school—to get started—but if so you need to be clear as to why you want to do what you want to do. If you don't do this, it's easy to see any such reason as a façade for simply wanting to go up in the *U.S. News* rankings.

As you are writing this do *not* include any of the reasons below in your Transfer Statement.

1. Any negative statements, or statements that could even be *perceived* as "bashing" your 1L school.

2. Merely wanting to move up in the rankings.

3. The 1L school's inability to challenge you intellectually. (See "bashing," above.)

4. More job opportunities for attending the transfer school. (See #2, above.)

Yes, the admissions dean and officers know why most transfer students are seeking to transfer. But try to persuade them with a more *legal* reason.

The Transfer Statement will not substitute for grades needed to qualify. Assuming you have those grades, however, the Transfer Statement is crucial to tipping your application into the *Yes* pile.

MULTIPLE SCHOOLS

With nearly anything involving law school, time is of the essence, and if you are sending applications out to multiple schools that means you will be sending multiple Transfer Statements as well. For the most part, you will not have to draft a completely new Transfer Statement for each school, but you will have to tailor each to address why you want to attend that law school. So, the "meat and potatoes" of your Transfer Statement can stay the same but what is going to be altered for each school is the experience, trait, or adversity you discuss tying into why you want to attend that specific school. However, be sure to check the school's website to verify that what you're submitting meets their requirements exactly. You will get no credit for being almost right.

HOUSEKEEPING

For any applications involving Early Action, you should mail the Transfer Statement directly to the schools. For other applications, you can simply upload it onto LSAC with the rest of the application (make sure your school takes transfer applications through LSAC). Also, double, triple, and quadruple check to make *sure* that you are sending the correct Transfer Statement to the corresponding law school. (It'll be tough gaining admission, regardless of your grades, if you foul this one up.)

RÉSUMÉ

Your résumé is the "e-you," your avatar. It is the first thing a law school sees, and it offers a summary of accomplishments. To highlight the important aspects of what a résumé should have, there are a few sample résumés at the end of this chapter to give you a visual aid. Put yourself in a law school's position. Do you want to see a résumé that entails a blank piece of paper with no qualifications? On the flip side, do you really want to go through a five-page résumé densely detailed with every achievement a potential candidate may have, especially if it lists "accomplishments" from middle school? I'm sure you are proud of that bicycle race you won or that spelling bee championship, but now is not the time to highlight such an achievement.

Likewise, unless your high school days were extraordinary (no, Al Bundy does not count as extraordinary), keep the high school glory days off the résumé. Résumés are about your most modern and substantive experiences, particularly in the field of law. Again, while you might have worked at Chuck-E-Cheese to help foot the bills, unless you're their general counsel or a supervisory manager, deans and admissions officers will have little interest in this information. The most they might want to see is some indication of initiative (as in paying your own bills), teamwork (as in working well with others), and problem-solving (as in highlighting a unique issue resolved). In sum, be aware of your audience and what they need to see.

The organization of your résumé should flow chronologically. First, put your contact information at the top of the page. Include all means of contacting you. This includes your address, email, and phone number. Your email address should be one you would feel comfortable sharing with your grandmother (assuming your grandmother is someone who would make an excellent, proper character in a *Masterpiece Theatre* miniseries).

This will most likely be the only uniform advice we can give. After your name and contact information, you need to decide whether your Education or Work Experience section will come next. Most of us will have our Education section listed first, as that's the most relevant at this point in our lives. This logically follows as up until now, the traditional twenty-one-year-old has more schooling than work experience. Start with law school and work your way back in time to your graduate school (if applicable) and undergraduate education. Do not list your high school. Each school should have its own section with its own detailed data. This should include your dates of attendance, your major (and minor) of study, your GPA, class rank, and your extra-curricular activities.

Your next section will be your Work Experience section. If you have a detailed work history, this is the time to be precise. If your work history is not so extensive, you might want to list community service or pro bono activities. Each job or pro bono activity should include the dates of employment or volunteer, the employers name and location, your position/title, and a brief description of what you did. Again, do this with the most recent job or volunteer activity first, and then work your way backwards in time. After those sections, try to highlight any other sections that will set you apart. If you have law or paralegal certifications, add that as a separate section. If you have been published, add that as a section and list your publications.

If you played a varsity sport in college or were in the military, these should be included. It is up to you in deciding where to place these experiences and accomplishments. For example, if you are applying to the law school where you played a varsity sport in undergrad, you might want to list this earlier in your résumé, perhaps below your education section. Be careful, however. Not everyone will perceive these in the same way. If this is an important experience, it might be worth crafting your Transfer Statement to explain why. Otherwise, it's generally best to list achievements and let them stand on their own, without drawing unnecessary attention to them.

In sum, make your résumé clear, powerful, and aesthetically pleasing. If an item is not of genuine substance, omit it. If you end up with mostly blank space, you'll need to think seriously about what exactly it is that you offer. What are your qualities, and how can you prove it?

LETTER OF ACADEMIC STANDING (DEAN'S CERTIFICATION LETTER)

The last piece to the application puzzle is the Letter of Academic Standing. This Letter contains the two most important bits of information a transfer law school wants to know about you. First, it contains your rank, which dictates to a law school how you performed in relation to the rest of your 1L class. Second, this letter states that you have completed your first year of law school in good academic standing. This means there are no disciplinary measures pending against you (such as accusations of cheating, missing forms, or any other potential incidents that could jeopardize your standing at your current law school).

These forms are in your school's Registrar's Office or on the school's website. You should request a Letter of Academic Standing, usually via the Registrar's Office, well in advance of the release of rank. Not only will you have handled the last piece to the puzzle, but it will give the Registrar's Office an opportunity to gauge how many letters they are going to have to prepare, as a separate letter must be drafted for each school for each student. Typically, the Letter will be drafted within 72 hours of rank being released. If you do reside in the city of your current law school at the time rank is issued, you should mail the letter yourself, with confirmation tracking. By mailing the letter yourself you will have peace of mind that they were sent, and you can track the letter.

INSIDE THE SECRET CHAMBER: A VIEW FROM ADMISSIONS

Here are recommendations as to many of the above technical issues from a law school dean of admissions:

Question: What factors, other than grades, are given the most attention when reviewing a transfer application?

Answer: While first-year grades remain the main factors, we also are interested in the applicant's ability to contribute to classroom dialogue and in the applicant's potential to contribute to scholarly research.

Question: Is the review process for transfer applications different than the review process for incoming 1L applications?

Answer: No, not very different.

Question: Are transfer applications decided by a single dean or a transfer committee?

Answer: A single dean, sometimes with the help of another faculty member.

Question: Do you see any detriments for admitting transfer students?

Answer: No.

Question: How does accepting transfer students benefit a law school? Academically? Financially? In terms of prestige or rankings?

Answer: Academically, new ideas and experiences spark the learning environment; financially, yes, additional revenue is generated; in terms of prestige or rankings, there's not much immediate effect.

Question: Why do you believe some schools are more transfer friendly than other schools?

Answer: It's possible that respective law school faculties vary in their willingness to have transfers join their classes.

Question: Do you believe the trend is for a continuing increase in the number of transfer applications?

Answer: It's hard to say, but my guess is yes, especially given the economy. (We are, as well, a public school.)

Question: Do you foresee the ABA stepping in and attempting to regulate the transfer process?

Answer: No.

Question: Besides the required materials (letters of recommendation, transfer statement, résumé) do you suggest transfer applicants include a writing sample? If so, should it be their entire appellate brief or the argument section extrapolated?

Answer: No, please no writing samples; we don't have time to read them.

Question: To facilitate the transfer process, do you prefer e-documents or paper documents when sending the required materials to a school?

Answer: Please use LSAC's e-app system.

Edward G. Tom is Assistant Dean for Admissions at the University of California–Berkeley Boalt Hall School of Law.

ADDITIONAL FAQS

If you get a deferral from a school that offers Early Action, do you have to resubmit a new application after spring grades are released?

No, all that is necessary to send is your official transcripts for both semesters along with a new Letter of Academic Standing that includes your class rank. You can submit supplemental materials, such as other letters of recommendation.

How much time is a fair amount of time to give a professor to write a letter of recommendation?

Generally, two weeks is an appropriate time. As two weeks are ending, if you've not gotten any confirmation you might check with the professor and cordially ask if they've had the chance to complete the letter. If there's any hesitation you can ask if they are likely to be able to complete it and, if not, you'll need to find an alternate. If there's any suspicion on your part that the professor is dragging his or her feet, now is the time to decide whether it's better to find another professor. The last thing you want is a perfunctory, ho-hum letter.

When is a good time to begin writing the Transfer Statement for Early Action? Regular Admissions?

The bad thing about Early Action is that you have to write your Transfer Statement while handling your Spring workload, which will be quite demanding. If you are that confident in your fall exams, then Winter Break is a good time. If not, wait until grades come out and then make the appropriate time with your focus still on your Spring classes. For Regular Admissions, start mapping out your Transfer Statement over Spring Break. Make sure to get started on it early in the summer. Sooner rather than later!

How do I switch my financial aid over from my Original 1L school to my 2L Transfer school?

When filling out the FAFSA form include your Original 1L school (just in case you do not transfer) along with your other top choices of schools to transfer to. This way if you get into one of the schools you listed your financial information will be sent to your 2L Transfer school.

How do I withdraw from my Original 1L school?

Notify your 1L Registrar *in writing* that you will not be attending that school anymore, and inform the Registrar of your New 2L Transfer school. Do *not* notify the Registrar at your Original 1L School before accepting an offer to attend your New 2L Transfer school.

– 4 –

Narrowing Your Schools

And you thought the hard part was over! Not just yet. Now comes the mind-boggling task of where to apply.

Yes, you have that one dream school that you are dying to get into. So, of course, you'll apply there. But what about others? For some, this part of the transfer process might feel almost more traumatic than your Civ. Pro. final. Careful thought should go into deciding which schools you have a realistic shot, sure shot, and long shot of getting into. Also, you should factor in your financial situation: how many schools you can afford to apply to? If your last name is Gates, okay, you might disregard this; for the rest of us, applying to law schools gets expensive, quickly.

For still others, this question might be easier. If you have your heart and mind set on a particular school—often one you didn't get accepted to for your 1L year—that's certainly an easy "decision" as to whether you'll apply there. But what if you do not get into that dream school? Do you have a Plan C? Or are you content with Plan A … your Original 1L School? Whether or not you think you have a "lock" to your dream school (which won't be the case, as this is a *transfer* application), as a future lawyer you should think in terms of contingency plans.

HOW TO NARROW YOUR SCHOOLS

If the only reason you are attempting to transfer law schools is to transfer to your dream school and that's it, great. You have saved yourself headache and time. Just get the application in on time with the appropriate required documents—and do them all very, very well—and then sit back and wait for your answer. For most of us, however, the necessity is that you are going to apply to more than one school. Some will apply to 3-4 and some could even apply to 10.

Okay then. Other than your dream school, which should you take a chance on, and how should you go about narrowing the other schools? Let's evaluate how to go about such a daunting task.

First, make a list of all the law schools you could see yourself at for your final two years. You can put down a school for any reason (yes, even if the reason is the university's football team, or nearby shopping district, or beaches, or whatever).

Finished? Let's move on.

Next take the list you just formulated and compare your final class rank percentage (x-axis) along with the tier of your Original 1L School (y-axis) and compare it to the chart below. This chart demonstrates to which schools you have the strongest likelihood of gaining acceptance. (We'll abbreviate Tier 1 to "T1," Tier 2 to "T2," and so on. Somewhat oddly, the Top 14 law schools are designated "T14," which of course is at the top of T1, rather than ten spaces below T4. We hope "top" and "tier" sharing the same "T" aren't too distracting.)

Law schools where your chances are good (a greater than 50% chance of admission) are listed in plain text. These are roughly analogous to the "safety" schools when you were applying as a 1L: you have a good chance to get in, although certainly no guarantee.

Law schools where your chances are not quite so strong, but which are likely where you want to focus your energies (a balance between higher-ranked schools and your chances of admission), are listed in **bold**. These are roughly analogous to the "target" schools when you were applying as a 1L. Those marked in **bold** are where your efforts (after grades) are most important: where acceptance will almost certainly be dependent upon on extraordinary positives in your well-written Transfer Statement, letters of recommendation, and otherwise.

Law schools where your chances are weak (a less-than-25% chance of admission), are shaded in gray. These are roughly analogous to your "dream" schools when you were applying as a 1L. If your other factors weigh towards applying, you should of course try—but it's important to know the odds.

		YOUR 1L RANK					
		Top 2%	Top 5%	Top 10%	Top 15%	Top 33%	Top 50%
ORIGINAL 1L SCHOOL	Tier 1	T14	**T14**	**T14** T1	**T14** T1	T14 **T1**	**T1**
	Tier 2	**T14**	T14 T1	T14 T1	T14 **T1**	T1 T2	T1 T2
	Tier 3	T14 T1	T14 **T1**	T14 T1 T2	T14 T1 T2	T1 T2 T3	**T2** T3
	Tier 4	T14 **T1**	T14 T1 T2	T14 T1 T2	T1 **T2**	T1 T2 T3	T2 T3

Official disclaimer: This chart does not, obviously, guarantee accept tance into a school that matches up with your class rank and Original 1L School tier. The chart should be used as a point of reference when narrowing your list of schools of where to apply. It might also be useful in giving an indication of just how steep the transfer application curve is.

Please keep in mind that law schools within each category will be vastly different when it comes to their overall approach to transfer students. During one transfer cycle (*i.e.,* one academic year), for example, Yale accepted 6 transfer students while Georgetown accepted 96; both are "officially" T14 schools. Moreover, a school toward the bottom of a tier can almost be in that lower tier; a school toward the top of a tier can almost be in the higher tier. This can complicate the above analysis.

No Tier 4 schools are listed in the chart as the assumption is that these would be lateral transfers.

LOOKING PAST GRADES

After crossing out schools where you do not feel you can make the grade cutoff—a crucial test—the logical progression is to look to five factors in yet another balancing test:

1. Rankings and prestige of New 2L School

2. Geography and employment "pull" of New 2L School

3. Programs, seminars, and clinics of New 2L School

4. Finances

5. Personal reasons

Rankings/Prestige. Many who consider transferring law schools do it for the same reason as everyone else: the chance to go to higher-ranked and more prestigious law school. There is a belief that the grass is greener on the other side, or the light at the end of the tunnel is much brighter, if you graduate from a higher-ranked law school. It's natural to look to the law school superstars—those T14 schools—and dream dreams of high-powered and prestigious law. You may be ashamed or feel slighted that you attend an "inferior" law school, or a sense that you were slighted in your applications, or a perceived need to attend the top school in your city, or just a nagging sense that you should be at a better law school.

Our perceptions and attitudes are important. When you go home for the holidays and are catching up with old friends and family members and they ask, "So, what are up to these days?"

Your answer might be a half-embarrassed or ho-hum "I'm in law school" instead of "Having a *great* time at Wow Law School!" Both responses get the message across, but there's a world of difference between the two, obviously. For some, the point of law school is, well, law school. For many others, there's a heavy shadow of just what that particular law school means, to you and to others: one day, when you're in that corner office, you'll want to feel proud of where you went to school and the diploma displayed in a place of honor on your wall.

Crucially, the ranking and prestige of your law school will play a pivotal role in landing your first job out of law school. This is true whether you land that job through the school's OCI process or through your own due diligence. And, of course, this is the not-so-secret reason many students are so serious about the transfer process—and why it's so important to take that process seriously.

Geography and employment pull. Rumor has it that going to a higher-ranked school or transferring to a school that is in the region you desire to practice will increase your chances of landing the job you wish to attain upon graduation. This rumor is true, and should be weighted heavily when narrowing where you plan to send transfer applications. Indeed, for this reason #1 (ranking and prestige) is closely tied to this factor. In a sense, geography is a fine-tuning of factor #1.

For most of us, we go to law school to become lawyers—as in practicing lawyers. (This might not be true for you, in which case this discussion and book might be even more important to your career hopes.) Dentists don't go to dental school to become accountants. Upon graduation nearly all of us will, therefore, be seeking a job in the legal field—whether that's our real desire or not. Thus, attending a law school in the geographic region you wish to be is a wise move. There's just one exception, really: if you attend a T14 law school, you can pretty much find a job wherever you want.

This is so important it bears repeating: if you're in a law school below the Top 14—yes, even in a Tier 1 (#15-50) school—chances are you will be limited in your search to jobs in the same area. This is not an absolute rule, of course. What it means is that your job search will be more difficult—sometimes *much* more difficult—outside the natural employment "pull" of that law school. Graduate from Harvard? We don't even have to write that you can find a job in Seattle as well as in Boston or New York City. Graduate from an East Coast law school in Tier 1 (but in the bottom of Tier 1)? Yes, you can find the job in Seattle, but it will probably take more work—perhaps even flying out yourself, at your own expense, to drum up an offer. Graduate from a far-away Tier 3 or Tier 4 law school? Good luck. Landing a job in Seattle will require a *lot* of work—and luck. We don't like this reality, but it is the truth—especially when the job market is bad.

Scenario 1 in Chapter 2 highlights the importance of this.

Programs, Seminars, and Clinics. This factor is relatively less important, but is still important to those who absolutely, positively know what type of law they want to practice. Again, this assumes that the practice area in question is not just a lark. For example, nearly everyone thinks "entertainment law" is sexy—and the few dozen lawyers who actually make a living practicing in this field would agree—but the real question is whether that follows a genuine interest. This interest should be backed by some real experience, or academic background, or *something*. This is not just for our purposes here—it will be on the minds of the admissions committee if it's a factor you focus on.

This factor can knock out a number of schools you might otherwise have been interested in attending because of factors #1 and #2. For this to be a factor for you, the law school in question needs not just to "have" a certain area of expertise, but to pride itself in that area and to have developed it with faculty, resources, and a long-term commitment and reputation. After all, the law school faculty will have certain expertise. If the school does focus in an area, they will hire additional faculty in that area, add focused seminars, clinics, and externships, and otherwise build an academic reputation in that area—all of which prospective employers will know.

As a 1L, you might not be aware of this focus, as it's primarily a concentration of advanced courses, seminars, and clinics you'll take in the next two years. The clinics especially, which are usually graded pass/fail—that's right, pass/fail—offer students real-world, "hands-on" experience, often with senior practitioners, judges, and visiting professors. These can be a fabulous way to build an inside track to a job—and a career—especially if that is your genuine area of interest.

If you are not one of the fortunate ones who knows exactly what kind of law you want to study—and this includes most of us—here's some good news. First, this factor won't weigh as heavily on you. Second, few employers will care; only those firms with specialized practices or with special needs will seek out graduates from those schools with known specialties. As a general rule, law firms seek top graduates from top schools, and assume that they'll train their new associates. The exceptions include firms practicing in intellectual property, where they might seek engineers or scientists who have focused in that area in law school, or environmental law firms, which likewise will seek those with technical backgrounds (usually) and an expressed interest and credentials (including seminars, clinics, externships, and so on).

Nonetheless, even if you're not sure you shouldn't simply overlook this factor. Law schools do need to focus their faculty recruitment in certain areas, so there should be a match between the school's emphasis and yours. Only in the largest law schools—often in the top one or two tiers—is there usually a focus in multiple areas, meaning that these large schools will have well-regarded clinical programs in multiple areas.

Spend some time, after spring finals are over, and do a little research on which are the well-established specialties of a law school you might apply to. How will you know if a program is "well established"? Not only will the law school tout it, but it will be listed elsewhere … *U.S. News,* specialized law journals and law practice sites, professors' blogs, and so on. You owe it to your future and to your wallet.

Finances. Show me the money! That's what most students might be secretly saying. It's also what law schools are saying when transfer season rolls around. Why is that? Well for starters, transfer applications bring in additional applications fees. With application fees ranging from $20-$100, these are not huge amounts of money but this does defray costs for the law school. These might pay for an extra staffer, or perhaps for part of an admission officer's salary.

How does this affect you? These application fees will add up quickly. If you're applying to just one dream school, chances are you'll get by with out-of-pocket costs of about $100. Most of us apply to more than one, so those costs add up: a few hundred dollars, easily. (There are also the LSAC fees to send your materials to each school.) Let's equate this to something tangible: perhaps a pair of Jimmy Choo shoes or a few nights out with your friends (or, if you're like us, *a* night out with your friends). This is a lot of money. Be sure that you're applying only to schools that you absolutely would be happy to attend. If not, don't waste your money.

If you find yourself planning to apply to a large number of schools: first, revisit the above question. Do you really, truly, honestly want to attend each and every one of those schools? If you're answer is that you're not sure, then think again and again about that school. You shouldn't throw money at something you'll end up either rejecting or regretting.

Second, request an application fee waiver. If legitimate, this can be the easiest way to save a *lot* of money and still apply to the schools you want. Please see Chapter 3: *The Application Process* for the subsection dealing with application fee waivers.

Personal reasons. This might be the trickiest and most amorphous part of your decision—yet it is likely to be among the most important.

In our lives, personal reasons such as family, a boyfriend or girlfriend (or a hoped-for boyfriend or girlfriend), or caring for others will take precedence over the factors above. Sometimes, it is a matter of practicality: without such a support system for you, or if you provide the support system for someone else, law school is impossible. Or, it can be a matter of desire: without that personal factor, law school (or life) seems pointless.

It's important to understand these reasons: we of course cannot cross-reference or even categorize these reasons with a particular school to which you might transfer ... but these reasons can weigh heavily in your decision. Our note of caution is that, understanding what your personal reason is, you not let that reason dictate your choice unreasonably. If it's for a set of practical constraints that simply keep you in that city, well, that's certainly understandable, and unavoidable. If, however, you're hoping for admission to a certain school to re-kindle a romance with a former boyfriend or girlfriend, think seriously before allowing such a "need" to dictate which schools you will (or will not) apply to.

Also, being happy (or at least comfortable) in the city where you will study (and likely practice) is important. You are already going to be walking into a new world of people, ideologies, and possibly weather, so the last thing you want to do is be in an uncomfortable environment that will not be conducive to your success.

CLOSING THOUGHTS ON CHOOSING THE RIGHT LAW SCHOOL

Your grades and the five factors presented in this chapter will to a large degree determine whether or not you can successfully transfer to a particular school. They should thus shape your final decision on where you choose to apply. You should, of course, "go for the gold" where you have a realistic shot to get in—if your personal reasons are aligned with that law school's qualities. And you should strive to improve and fine-tune your application to the extent that you have at least a decent shot even at your dream school.

These discussions and scenarios and factors will help you in making a better transfer application, and also in focusing better on the right law schools for you. Some factors can and should weigh more heavily on your mind than others; overlooking one without giving it the attention it deserves can, however, be detrimental in your successful transfer to the very best law school for you.

TRANSFER STATISTICS FOR SELECTED LAW SCHOOLS

Here's a chart of law schools responding to our inquiries about the transfer process. This might not seem terribly helpful—especially if a school you're interested in is not listed—but in fact some of this information can be quite difficult to obtain, and is certainly tedious to obtain. So, we offer it as both a sense of how accepting each tier of law school is with regard to transfer applications, generally, and also for specific data if a law school you are interested in is listed:

LAW SCHOOL	NO. OF APPS	NO. OF OFFERS	STUDENTS ACCEPTING	SUCCESS RATE	% OF STUDENTS ACCEPTING
Yale Univ.	N/A	N/A	12	N/A	N/A
Harvard Univ.	200	35	30	18%	86%
Stanford Univ.	150	12	12	8%	100%
Univ. of California–Berkeley	200-250	53	45	25%	85%

LAW SCHOOL	NO. OF APPS	NO. OF OFFERS	STUDENTS ACCEPTING	SUCCESS RATE	% OF STUDENTS ACCEPTING
Univ. of Michigan–Ann Arbor	175	53	32	30%	60%
Univ. of Virginia	214	21	20	10%	95%
Duke Univ.	104	36	19	35%	53%
Washington Univ. in St. Louis	160	67	38	42%	57%
George Washington Univ.	325	103	66	32%	64%
Emory Univ.	63	31	18	49%	58%
Fordham Univ.	300	70	30	23%	43%
Univ. of Illinois–Urbana –Champaign	134	30	24	22%	80%
Univ. of Iowa	18	12	8	67%	67%
Univ. of Washington	50	5	2	10%	40%
Univ. of Alabama	N/A	N/A	11	N/A	N/A
Indiana Univ. Bloomngton	50	3	3	6%	100%
Univ. of Wisconsin	45	24	15	53%	63%
George Mason Univ.	111	7	2	6%	29%
Univ. of Arizona	30	13	7	43%	54%
Univ. of North Carolina (Chapel Hill)	58	7	7	12%	100%
Wake Forest Univ.	50	20	15	40%	75%
Tulanc Univ.	65	30	22	46%	73%
Univ. of California–Davis	103	30	12	29%	40%
Univ. of Connecticut	39	15	12	38%	80%
Univ. of Florida	120	27	20	23%	74%
Univ. of Utah	39	21	13	54%	62%
Arizona State Univ.	67	24	19	36%	79%

Law School	No. of Apps	No. of Offers	Students Accepting	Success Rate	% of Students Accepting
Univ. of Cincinnati	25	22	16	88%	73%
Univ. of Tennessee–Knoxville	9	0	0	0%	N/A
Brooklyn Law School	200	50	24	25%	48%
Loyola Marymount Univ.	227	75	41	33%	55%
Seton Hall Univ.	111	48	19	43%	40%
Univ. of New Mexico	17	9	6	53%	67%
Univ. of Pittsburgh	32	17	11	53%	65%
Georgia State Univ.	93	8	8	9%	100%
Rutgers–Newark	142	25	14	18%	56%
Loyola Univ.–Chicago	64	29	11	45%	38%
Univ. of Hawaii	13	3	2	23%	67%
Univ. of Miami	93	19	6	20%	32%
Univ. of San Diego	143	40	20	28%	50%
Marquette Univ.	N/A	N/A	14	N/A	N/A
Univ. of South Carolina	40	20	18	50%	90%
Mercer Univ.	34	8	8	24%	100%
Univ. of Buffalo at SUNY	71	35	32	49%	91%

This is data for the 2008 entering 2L year. Each law school might alter its transfer admissions policy, of course. We thus plan to periodically update this information, which our publisher has agreed to provide on its website (www.fineprintpress.com).

5

GRADES

In every aspect of life, performance is judged by some quantifiable number or letter that illustrates how well or how poorly you have done. This measurement is often used to compare that performance against the performance of the rest of the field. This we call competition.

In sales, a salesperson is judged by how much revenue is brought in for the company or how many products are sold in a certain period. In sports, an athlete is judged by how many points are scored in a game or how fast from point A to point B or how many passes/goals/etc. are achieved. In television, shows are judged by how many viewers watch the show.

In law school, especially in your first year of law school, students are judged squarely on the grades they earn. Just like the salesperson who brings in the most revenue or sells the most product, or the athlete who scores the most points or runs the fastest, or the television show that garners the highest ratings, the rewards for finishing at the top of your 1L class can be just as lucrative. From opening the doors to the country's most prestigious law schools, to being competitive in the law firm recruitment process, high grades in your 1L year can and will be your "golden ticket."

UNDERSTANDING THE CURVE

For those not yet in law school, please allow us to explain the infamous law school curve. (If you are in law school, you'll know just why this is "infamous.")

Yes, you might be familiar with "the curve" by having had curved courses in your undergraduate courses. But, chances are, you haven't faced a curve quite like the one you will in law school. Only in the hard sciences (usually), does the grade curve even begin to approach the one in law school.

The Curve is the mean GPA set by the law school. This curve is mandated: professors are *required* to follow it in apportioning their grades. Every school has a different curve, but as you move down in the rankings The Curve becomes increasingly harsh. For example, if a law school sets its curve at a 3.0, this means (no pun intended) the average GPA of your section will be 3.0. Half above and half below.

Additionally, some law schools impose harsher restrictions on professors as to how many of each grade can be given. For example, only a certain percentage of grades may be an A, or A grades versus B and C grades, or A grades versus C grades, or some such. Even if no restrictions are mandated, a law professor apportions the grades *so long as the mean GPA results in a 3.0.*

This still doesn't sound too bad, right?

Take a section of 100 students with The Curve set at a 3.0, with no restrictions on the professor as to specific grade ratios. The professor might give 50 "A's" and 50 "C's", which will of course produce the required mean of 3.0. Not too likely. Or the professor might give 1 "A", 98 "B's", and 1 "C", producing the same, required 3.0 mean. More likely is a curve something along these lines: 10-20 "A's" and "A-'s"; 60-70 "B's" 10-20 "C's," and 5-10 "D's" and "F's." And that's if the school follows a 3.0 mean; many require a lower mean.

We'll get right to the point: if you aren't in the first category of those with "A" grades, your chances of transferring law school are remote. The more you hope to transfer to a law school ranked significantly better than your Original 1L school, the better your grades have to be. To break into the Top 14, your grades need to be described not as top x% (and certainly not top xx%), but rather as #z in the class: your class rank, or z/zzz. That's how stiff the competition is—and that's how seriously the dean will be looking at your transfer application.

The good news? Your grade *is* something you can control. It is within your power to "convert" your LSAT and undergraduate GPA to relatively minor considerations in your (second) application to your dream school. A showing as, say, 2/345, or second-highest student in a class of 345 1L students, almost certainly will carry significant weight. That so-so LSAT and unimpressive GPA become a little less important than your stellar standing which shows that you can *already do* what the admissions committee is asking whether you can do: succeed in law school

Importantly, many students become so concerned with The Curve that they allow it to take them away from valuable study time. Do not fall into this trap. Do not get consumed on how many A's and B's can, will, or are able to be given out. Who cares?! You will get only ONE grade in each course, and that grade has to be an "A." The only way The Curve will affect you in a negative way is if you let it. Do not be distracted, and do not focus on it. Absolutely do not let it consume you. Instead of using the time to research who can get what grades, or run statistical models in your head of just what combinations will lead to a certain result, use the time to STUDY!

We'll provide more tips later. For now, please remember that law school exams test you on your knowledge of the law and on your ability to apply that knowledge, not how well you know the law school's grading policies.

SIZING UP THE COMPETITION

It's human nature to size up your opposition—to try to understand just what you're up against. In ancient times this might have been how strong the other side looked, or how sharp the spear was. In school, it's all about how smart we are. In law school, it's about how smart *everyone* is.

As we need to judge the competition before performance can even be judged, this leads us to use stereotypes from past experiences. In law school, we thus size up our competition through the old measurements—class participation, number of hours you might see someone in the library, the amount of study supplements one student has over you, or involvement in extracurricular activities. You can (and will) play a host of mind games on yourself. All of these lead … nowhere. The only positive is if these motivate you to forget sizing your competition up and instead simply compete. In most cases, however, we look to these measurements and realize, too late, that we've been measuring the wrong things in law school. If channeled properly, the energy you use to assess the competition should be used as a source of motivation. It is this motivation that, if properly focused, will help you to perform to the peak of your abilities...and above everyone else's, or nearly everyone else.

At the end of the day (or, more correctly, at the end of your first year), all of those measurements will have absolutely nothing to do with the respective performance of each of your classmates, or for you. These are all simply irrelevant to law school grades, which are determined by (sorry to repeat ourselves here) your knowledge of the law and on your ability to apply that knowledge. So whatever category or classification you begin to divide your competition into, being in one or the other does not provide any indication on how well or how poorly one will do in law school.

Okay. What *will* help?

Here are ways to actively motivate yourself:

The Gunner. Most law students are overachievers. Most overachievers have attempted to impress power figures their whole lives—literally. From kindergarten on, some students simply have to show how bright and connected they are to the teacher. Take for instance a classmate who feels the need to raise his or her hand and answer every question in class to justify an overwhelming intellect. Instead of mumbling under your breath on how annoying the person is after the 28th interjection or your urge to tell him to "Give it up already!" (or worse), think of a way to counter his argument. Remember in class: as a law student and soon-to-be-lawyer it is your job to see both sides to every issue. If you feel it necessary to stand up and say it in class, then do so. Better, however, is simply to engage in a silent debate with every speaker. Are they right? If not, why not? If partially right, why? Under what conditions would the answer change? And so on.

If anything, it will be better to present (or ask about) a counterargument after class with the professor, one-on-one. Not only will this help build a rapport with your professor for a possible letter of recommendation, but it will give you some insight on how the professor perceives other arguments that may invariably help you out come test time when you have to argue both sides of an issue. There is no magic to exams: they test your ability to understand and construct logical, legal reasoning.

The Loner. At times you may be annoyed with peers who seem tucked away in a corner, studying away. But remember, they have the same goal as you. In essence you are not really annoyed with them; you're questioning whether *you* are putting in the appropriate amount of time and effort to get the high grades to land yourself at the law school of your dreams. The one question we have for you is: will you regret it if you did not put in that extra hour or two a day to get the grades you truly want? (And, *ahem,* the grades you need to transfer to your dream school.) If the answer is no, then you have nothing to worry about, but if you believe you will have doubt when you get your grades back and see a "B" on your transcript in Civil Procedure and not an "A," will you regret not working that extra hour a day? This, by the way, adds up over a semester to a whole work week of learning time. (And that's a mere 40 hours, not a lawyer's work week of 60-80 hours.)

> Fortunately enough for me, as with all law schools my school had mid-terms for the majority of the classes at the end of my 1L fall semester. This was a way for us to get used to the law school testing format. Even though the test only counted for about 10-20% of the grade, it was extremely beneficial for me to hone in on my test-taking skills.
>
> About two weeks prior to mid-terms I decided to start coming to school at 7:00 a.m. Monday through Friday, as opposed to the usual 9:00 a.m. start time I was accustomed to. Not knowing if the extra study time was going to help my chances on the exams, I was willing to make the sacrifice to see if my efforts paid off. This decision was motivated by two reasons: (1) my drive to transfer to the best law school I could get into; and (2) a girl I saw in the library every time I walked in. Not knowing what effect the extra 20 hours of study time would provide, I was relieved to see my three mid-term grades: 2nd, 4th, and 5th–highest in the class.
>
> From then on, I was at school from 7:00 a.m., five days a week, for the rest of the spring semester.

The Supplement King (or Queen). After figuring out where all your classes are, trying to find a good seat, meeting new friends, creating social circles, getting a feel for your professors, and learning a completely new style of writing, now comes the task of attempting to learn and understand the material taught.

One way of learning the material is to purchase supplements. Supplements to the readings provide two things: (1) a way of short-cutting your reading to get the meat and potatoes of what is going on; and (2) a way of learning the material in a different form to help facilitate your knowledge of what is going on.

At times, law students will become overwhelmed with which supplements to buy and which are better than the other. Some students resort to not using supplements because they feel they don't need them, or simply cannot afford them. Whatever the case, do not allow another student to psyche you out because you have not purchased as many supplements, or you have purchased too many, or whatever. This is utterly and completely beside the point. Getting caught up in which supplements to purchase over the others will only distract you from your goal of obtaining top-notch grades. That follows from learning the law, which follows from cases, texts, and, yes, supplements. But the quantity of supplements, or the quality of such-and-so actual brand-name ... those are a dead end, and a waste of your time.

To be more specific in deciding which supplements are better for your needs:

1. Pay attention. If your professor brings a supplement to class, or uses a supplement in his or her office—that's probably a good bet. It's certainly not going to hurt. Most likely, they use these supplements not only to help with their understanding of the fine points of the law but they might also be plucking or tweaking hypos from the supplement for a potential test question. *Bingo!* Also, a visit to their office might help, as professors tend to have books lying around their office or up on shelves, which they may have used or referred to in the past. Ask them about these. Are they good? Did they explain first-year concepts well? Is there an example from a recent class?

2. Take advantage of advice given in the syllabus as to which supplements the professor recommends.

3.   Become friendly with other 2Ls and 3Ls. Ask them if they had your professor, and what they used. Don't be shy. You might, in your conversation, get a sense of how well they did in that class. This is important, of course, but don't be too quick to discount advice from someone who didn't do well. After all, we often learn the most from our mistakes. So pay attention. 2Ls and 3Ls are a wealth of information. Most likely someone helped them out and they are looking to return the favor.

4.   Check the law school library. It probably has a wide selection of supplements in each field. Some might be older, but don't worry too much; supplements tend to change only with fast-changing topics (such as some field in constitutional law that's recently undergone a judicial upset). Choose a single course subject. Choose a single topic within that subject that you're studying *that week*. Get every supplement they have. Read each supplement on that topic. Take your time. Read each one, again. Which one helped you the most? That's the one you might buy.

The Mayor. Some first-year students take an active role in the various groups and organizations at law school. From Student Bar Association ("SBA") membership to the American Bar Association ("ABA") to specific practice area membership groups—for example, the John Marshall Bar Association, Entertainment and Sports Law Society, National Black Law Students Association—these groups and organizations can provide a great social outlet to the rigors of law school and be a decent résumé builder. These activities will be a mistake, however, if they are a distraction in your attempt to get the best possible grades.

Social activities, such as after-hour get-togethers can be a great way to blow off steam and a good way to build camaraderie with your future colleagues. If you are interested in these, be sure not to overdo it. These are great *in moderation*. They are grade-killers, in excess. Most importantly, you really don't have time in your first year to squander on these distractions—save it for later.

Clubs and organizations also provide an opportunity for students to network with future colleagues and an opportunity to meet practitioners. Attaining the proper balance between social desires and your class workload is important. As you no doubt know already, time management in your first year of law school is almost more difficult than the actual law you learn (well, maybe except for Future Estates and the Rule Against Perpetuities).

Too much involvement in any organization (or, needless to say, in a multitude of organizations) in an attempt to "beef up" your résumé could—will—distract you from your main focus: getting the best grades you can. Every hour spent on some extracurricular activity is an hour you sacrifice from your real "job"—learning the law.

To be clear, we're not saying not to get involved in any organizations at your law school. We are saying that you should remember what *needs* to be done to attain your goal of transferring, because when you apply to transfer, law schools are more interested in your performance in the classroom than your ability to plan a happy-hour social. Moreover, once you do get into your dream transfer school, you can and should spend a bit of that socializing time to get to know your new 2L colleagues.

TO DISCUSS GRADES OR NOT TO DISCUSS GRADES

Upon the release of Fall grades at the beginning of the Spring semester, the chatter as to who got what and who booked what will try to consume you, and yes it will try. The question is: will you allow it? This topic is, to many in your 1L class, bigger than nearly any other question. Even juicy rumors about who is hooking up with whom in your section (or from other sections) is pushed to the side as your classmates attempt to see how they stack up against each other. All real-world news and events go out the window upon the release of these grades, and it is hard to stay out of the Chatter.

In answering the inevitable question, "How'd you do?" there are many different approaches. Many are reticent to discuss how they fared on their exams—given the grade curve, nearly everyone feels that their grades should have been higher. Many have not gotten a "B" (much less a "C") in years … if ever. If you earned "A's" and one "B" and you tell someone that's what you got, you'll be perceived as bragging. If you got straight "C's," your insecurities will bubble to the surface. For the most part, people will thus answer the grades question with an "I did okay" or a "Not too bad, I could have done a little better," which, at the end of the day, provides no feedback to those on the quest of finding out who is at the top of the class.

With that being said, the decision is up to you whether you want to discuss your grades or not. If you choose to discuss your grades with someone in your section, be prepared once you tell one person that you will be placing not only your whole section on notice of what you received but the rest of the 1L class. Especially if you did well, information relating to grades spreads like wildfire. By telling just one person you have just "gone public" with how you match up with everyone else in the class, and the comparisons and criticisms will commence. If you did well and you do tell people exactly what you earned, be prepared for the parade of questions to come your way on your thoughts about the previous exams (as it is hard—very hard—for some people to just let go), study habits you found successful, multiple offers to be a part of study groups, and attempts by other students to try and knock you off your game. (Remember, it is still a competition, and some will take this competition very, very seriously. You should as well, for different reasons.)

Bottom line advice: do not discuss grades. It's no one's business, and there's no winning this discussion. If you want to keep your performance to yourself, then give the typical answer of "I did okay" or even "Just a warm-up to Spring!" and for the most part when others see that you are not willing to give up the specific grades then the questions will stop. (You cannot, of course, ask about *their* grades without being expected to divulge your own.) If you do choose to discuss your grades with others, you'll bask in the warm glow of adulation—but you'll also become the target for sniping. It's just human nature. This is especially true when someone does unexpectedly well. But remember, the old "skills" of study in undergraduate school will have almost no relevance to those you need to employ in law school. Thus, many "A" students *do* come as a surprise to their classmates … they've been studying smart. It's easy for others to see this as somehow unjust—but this person never even spoke in class!—and thus there's a bad combination of envy, jealously, and conspiracy. Avoid this. Do not discuss grades.

Some like the thrill of being asked to tutor others. Be very, very careful. You still have work to do, and the Fall grades do not count (much)—it's the Spring grades that will be crucial. Maintain your focus! In general, you should find those who are as willing to give (meaning study hard and engage in a real discussion), rather than those who are simply clueless. Studying the law means, to a large extent, learning it on your own. These interactions are to confirm and fine-tune that knowledge, but the bulk of the responsibility is on you and you alone. Maintain your focus.

WHAT TO DO WHEN FALL GRADES COME OUT

Nobody—and we mean *nobody*—has any idea if they have a realistic chance of transferring until fall grades come out. Once grades come out, you can now assess your realistic chances of which law schools you have a shot of getting into.

If you plan on applying to a school that has an Early Action program, such as the University of Chicago, Georgetown University Law Center, Washington University of St. Louis, or Boston College, you should begin to get a start on all the legwork (letters of recommendation, transfer statement, etc.) as soon *as you get your grades.* This means immediately! Don't wait. If you do choose to make this move you will be announcing to the school that you have intentions on transferring, because you are going to have to request a Letter of Good Standing and a copy of your official transcripts from the Registrar's Office, which will include your GPA and class rank. The majority of times when a student requests this kind of information from the Registrar's office, it is to transfer. They're not going to get mad, but you do need to be prompt. For the most part, schools are pretty good at getting the Letter of Academic Standing to you in a timely manner; like anything in life, however, unforeseen obstacles do occur. If you do have a strong intention to transfer, get this request in as early as possible as deadlines will approach in early February to get the required materials to the transfer schools.

You will also need to talk to professors, give them time and help in completing the letters of recommendation. You want to give yourself as much time as possible if anything goes wrong, which means that you need to start as early as possible. That means immediately. Do not wait.

As to how to send the these materials to the school, we suggest that you send both the Letter of Good Standing and copy of your Official Transcript together directly to the Early Action law schools you are applying to. The second option is to use the LSAC, but this is not recommended:

1. The transfer application process is one that involves a tight timeframe. You thus want to cut out any avoidable delays, including those of a third party. LSAC generally does a good job, but who knows? It's better to mail and confirm your own documents, so that there's no question. (It's definitely worth paying for tracking of your mail or packets. Yes, this may cost a little extra, but will be well worth it in the long run if you can get into one of these schools.) Remember, we are dealing with a potential life-changing event.

2. If a regular transfer application has a tight timeframe, an Early Action application has an *extremely* tight timeframe. Be sure that every document needed is sent and received. It's not done until you've confirmed that it's done.

3. Your current law school may offer to send these documents, but it may be difficult for you to find out when they were sent, thus distracting you and taking time away from your studies. And if somehow they weren't sent, you might waste a precious week (or more) to find that out.

4. Amidst the potential horror stories of law schools delaying the sending of documents, it's best to just eliminate such a possibility and simply mail them yourself if you can.

As to the other materials that accompany your application (application, application fee, transcripts from your previous institutions), these can all be sent through the LSAC service.

GOING 2 FOR 2: PRODUCING THE SAME OR BETTER IN THE SPRING

As a potential transfer student, when your Fall grades come out in the beginning of your spring semester, one can assume you are either trying to maintain the same level of performance or improve upon your Fall performance. How to accomplish this? The truth is that, after Fall grades come out and people begin to see where they stack up amongst the others, the competition for the top grades only increases.

If you are fortunate enough to do well in the fall, you may breathe a sigh of relief—but only momentarily. Compared to the others in your section, you've "got it," meaning you understand the basic principles on how take a law school exam, and are able to best dictate your answers in a coherent manner that is easy for the professor to read and you get to the point through your analysis of the legal issue. In other words, you know how to think like a lawyer. The bad news: now everyone is gunning for what you have accomplished.

The idea of grades—and the aforementioned grade curve—do not become *real* to law students until they actually see their first-semester grades, first-hand. For the most part, after taking your first law exams you have no clue on how you fared. You could think that you dominated an exam and end up with a "C+," or you might believe you bombed an exam and land a "B+."

If you are in the fortunate boat of being towards the top of your class after fall grades have been released, here's what we recommend: act as if someone is trying to take something very, very important away from you. It is as if someone is literally coming into your house and taking away a tangible item of yours that you hold near and dear to your heart (it could be a loved one, a lifelong pet, a flat-screen television, whatever). Use the motivation of others to re-motivate yourself to keep what you have already accomplished. Your Fall grades serve only to push you to do better then what you even thought was possible … as your peers are attempting to take down from your wall a Juris Doctor diploma with a name on it from the law school of your dreams.

If, however, you have to make the up-hill climb because the Fall semester did *not* turn out as well as you had anticipated, this is the time to embrace a new challenge. Think about what you did in preparation for your fall exams. If you did a lot of talking, note-taking, cramming, and so on ... stop. Use this as a lesson, and take it one step at a time:

1. First, re-read your exams, carefully, and analyze what mistakes you made. What issues did you miss? What legal tests? What prongs from those tests? What exceptions or quirks might you have included?

2. After you have re-read your exams seriously, discuss with the professors what you might have done to improve. For the most part, professors are all looking for the same thing: they want to see a lawyer "talking" to them, through the exam. If your exam included multiple choice or short-answer questions, the same thought process applies as it would to the essay portion. Did you jump to conclusions? Did you insert unnecessary facts? What, specifically, did you miss?

3. Do not be satisfied with generalities. You want to know EXACTLY why you missed each point. This is the first step to getting those points in your next set of exams ... in the spring.

4. Ask yourself, what study techniques did you find were most effective? If you didn't do well, be honest. Were you *really* studying? Were you really *learning* anything when you were studying? (The book *Law School: Getting In, Getting Good, Getting the Gold* addresses this point.)

5. Remember that your Fall semester is your first taste of law school. Now that you have that semester under your belt, you can better approach the Spring semester as you no longer are in the trial-and-error phase of the process.

6. This may be intimidating, but if you do know of a student who did well, pull that person aside and ask them how they studied for the exam and what they found effective in learning the material as compared to what they felt was ineffective. Stories of students not helping each other is a myth. Yes, there are those not willing to

help, but most will. (And you should too.) You will never know unless you ask.

7. Find a 2L or 3L who did well—such as those on law review—and ask them the same question.

8. One more time. *Be honest with yourself.* Did you really put in the time and effort to get that "A"? Could you have stayed in a couple of Thursday, Friday, or Saturday nights to master the concepts of consideration or vicarious liability? Just remember, every night that you go out you not only lose the time of studying that evening, but will most likely not be as efficient the next day because of the late night before.

In an attempt to improve your grades and stay on track with your current grades, here are some hints:

1. If you choose to get a supplement, we suggest the *Examples and Explanations* series, as they provide an in-depth explanation of the topic and numerous examples with detailed answers. Usually a few hundred pages, these cover most, if not all, of the topics in your class. They're written with introductory sections and useful background information. This is vital as it provides the framework for the rules you need to learn—black letter law—and then apply on your exams. Further, these books include examples and problems for you to try to apply the rule of law you just learned. After each example there is an explanation (thus the series title), with a model answer and analysis of the answer. These examples are vital as they allow you to apply the rules of law you learned to various patterns. Reading the E&E before reading the cases will allow you to focus more on what is going on in the case then trying to master the concept from the case. You will find it much easier to comprehend not only the facts of the case but how the rule of law is being applied to the facts because you have already introduced yourself to the rule before reading the case.

2. We know this sounds difficult, but try to have *all* of your reading done for all of your classes two weeks before finals start. With reading out of the way, you now have

to focus only on finishing your brief, memo, or oral argument, and mastering the concepts for the exam. During this two-week period, you should attempt to do as many practice multiple choice and essay questions as possible. Practice makes perfect and the only way you are going to improve upon last semester's performance is to take the concepts and apply them to as many different types of situations as possible. Look to:

a. *Questions and Answers.* This supplement is a workbook jam-packed with multiple choice questions that are separated by topics in their respective subject of law.

b. *Law in a Flash.* These break the flash cards into topics of the class. In each topic, the first five or so flash cards will introduce you to the black letter law while the rest of the cards will give you hypothetical fact patterns and ask you the result. On the back of the flash card is a model answer and explanation.

c. *Audio Immersion.* CDs. This is a great way to kill two birds with one stone: you can be doing more than one activity while studying at the same time. Going to the gym to lift weights or going on that 5-mile run, or just commuting, you can still study and make the time pass by quicker while listening to Law CDs on your PDA.

3. One technique that can be highly rewarding—and helpful in mastering the law—is tutoring.

After the release of Fall grades, I was one of the fortunate ones to have finished in the top 5% of my class. I am not going to lie that that sense of accomplishment felt great, but only for a moment. I thought to myself, how did I do so well? I know I had put the needed time and effort in, but had I guessed right on a couple of multiple choice questions or did I attack an issue in a way that no one in my class thought of? I knew that the competition was only going to increase and my peers were going to step their game up.

I was trying to think of ways to mix up my studying so it did not become monotonous, and then one day, one of my classmates approached me, and without his knowing provided me with the answer I was looking for. Richard, a student who did not fare as well as he imagined in the fall semester, approached me after Contracts class one day and asked me if I could help tutor him. It dawned on me that if I could teach the material to a fellow class-mate with little or no use of my notes, it would provide me with more confidence going into the exam. Throughout the year Richard and I would have weekly study sessions going over Respondeat Superior one day, and the Commerce Clause the next day. While on other days we covered topics such as assigning rights to a contract and landlord/tenant relationships. As the year winded down, our sessions began to increase and my mindset for studying shifted from not only preparing myself for the exams, but as if I had an obligation to come into the tutoring sessions with Richard knowing the material inside and out. That obliga-tion provided an extra boost to my drive not only for myself to succeed in law school but to help one of my peers succeed as well.

WHAT TO DO WHEN SPRING GRADES COME OUT

At last, your Spring grades have finally all been posted and you are now able to view your first-year law school GPA. At this moment, you are either elated, disappointed, devastated, or just extremely nervous. You play countless head games with yourself and map out all different scenarios. Regardless of where you are mentally, you might be saying to yourself, "Well, I have my grades, but what I real-ly need is my class rank, because the rank is going to be used as the true measure of how I stacked up against everyone in my class."

This is true and if your school is one that does not post grades with rank simultaneously you are in a bit of a holding pattern, but there are still a number things you can do during the time you are (anxiously) awaiting your rank.

1.　Double-check to make sure the schools you are applying to have received all other materials for your application (completed application, application fee, letters of recommendation, Transfer Statement, any addendums). This means all they are waiting for is your class rank (which will be stated in your Letter of Academic Standing) to make a decision.

2. Put in your requests for your first-year school to send the official transcripts to the schools you are applying to. It is okay to send your official transcripts without yet knowing your rank, because you can request your ranking to be included in your Letter of Good Standing. When requesting your official transcripts there will likely be a fee for each. Try to pay the transcript fees online via credit card, as it is an easier mode to confirm, pay, and keep your records in order.

3. Print a copy of your unofficial transcript and either fax or mail it to the schools you are applying to so they can have your grades on file. The schools will probably not make an official decision on your file, but may position your application differently now that they know your final GPA and can compare it to past applicants from your Original 1L School.

4. Attempt to request an estimated ranking from your school based on previous year's GPA's, so that you can provide the school(s) you are applying to an approximation on where you stand.

5. Have all of your requests for Letters of Academic Standing filled out and organized, so that you can drop them off immediately after the release of rankings.

6. *Politely* call your first-year's registrar's office to find out when the anticipated release date for the rankings is. (This is one of the visits or calls you make to help develop a friendly rapport with the registrar's office as they are the ones who will be drafting your Letter of Academic Standing). This is important because along with sending your unofficial transcript along with an approximate ranking based on the previous year's numbers, you will be able to inform the schools you are applying to when your official ranking will be known.

WHAT TO DO ONCE RANKINGS ARE POSTED

Finally, finally, the most important number in your transfer application—your first-year class rank—is posted. No more "he got these grades," or "she got those grades" in fleeting attempts to jostle mentally with your peers. This sets, almost in concrete, just where each stands.

Now the race begins to get your ranking to the schools as quickly as possible: the deadlines are looming. As mentioned above, it can only help you by building a relationship with personnel who work in your first-year school's Registrar's office, especially if you are coming from a school where a lot of students are attempting to transfer out. It's human nature that people will feel more inclined to help others who are nice and respectful to them rather than demanding, insensitive, or rude.

Here are a few ways that rapport can be built in a law school Registrar's office (and everywhere else, come to think of it):

1. Remember everyone's name. Everyone likes to hear their own name. Everyone loves to hear you remember their name. This shows that you valued meeting them and that they garner respect from you. Such a useful trait helps when you see someone passing you in the halls, and you can say more than just "Hiya."

2. As in many businesses, the office personnel such as secretaries and mail room staff are *always* "in the know" with what's going on. They handle the day-to-day operations, after all. (Don't ever think you can pull one over on a staffer.) The same is true in a law school, so it may behoove you to drop in every once in a while to say hello and ask how their day is going. (A friend of mine received a partial scholarship at his law school by doing just this: not one person applied for it, and one of the front office personnel asked if he was interested in applying since no one else had.)

3. Do *not* send gifts, flowers, food baskets, etc. In your mind it might be just a thoughtful gesture and a *thanks* for the Registrar's hard work over the summer to get the grades posted as quickly as possible, but it can be perceived by

others in a negative light—a bribe of sorts. A simple, in-person *thank you* or card after you have already been accepted to your new school will do.

It sounds elementary, but be cognizant at all times of how you interact with everyone. Not only in the Registrar's office, but everywhere, all the time. Staff do talk, and you don't want your name coming up in connection with a negative comment.

Not only is it wise to try and set yourself apart from the rest of the applicants in your application to potential transfer schools through your Transfer Statement, but it is wise as well to separate yourself among others from your first-year law school with the front office personnel in the Registrar's office. Coming from a school where there may be as many as 10-30 students attempting to transfer, the workload on the Registrar's office increases with each request. Furthermore, every potential transfer applicant is more than likely not just applying to just one or two schools. If an average applicant sends out 4-8 applications—which means that for every school two documents are going out to each—this means that potentially hundreds of letters need to be sent. It is therefore in your best interest (as well as ethical interest) to befriend those and create strong professional relationships as early as possible.

[Editor's note: This is exactly the same standard that applies in the practice of law.]

DELAYS: CONTESTING A GRADE

After anxiously awaiting the arrival of spring grades and pulling your hair out each time you check your school's website—followed by checking the date to see how dangerously close you're getting to the application-complete deadline, the grades all post. You breathe a sigh of relief ... but now comes a sense of panic. One or two of the grades stick out like a sore thumb. These are the grades that shock you and create a huge knot in your stomach. You've already added to the inordinate stress on yourself to do well in your first year. What if you get a bad grade?

If you feel that you really bombed an exam then you have a different problem, but if you genuinely feel that there's no conceivable way you could have earned that bad grade, you need to act fast. With class rank impending and deadlines looming, how do you handle this seemingly insurmountable obstacle before the schools' deadlines?

1. There's the ever-important first rule: don't panic. This might be the hardest obstacle to overcome, because your mind is racing around the issue of how you can "fix" a seemingly unfixable problem before your class rank comes out *and* before a school can make a decision on your application.

2. As a first step to actually fixing the problem, email your professor to arrange a time to meet, to go over your exam to see where they deducted points. If your professor is unavailable because he or she was a visiting professor or is out of the country or is simply not available, attempt to arrange a meeting with the head of the department to review your exam. After this meeting, take a day to consider whether you genuinely have a strong case to contest the grade. Discuss the issue with others, perhaps, but in the end it is a gut-check: is it really, truly, a wildly inaccurate grade?

3. Read and analyze the section on grade appeals in your school's Code of Conduct to make sure you understand how the process works and what standard of error you must prove that your test was graded improperly by your professor. In nearly all cases, it is analogous to the standard that an appellate court applies to trial courts: it is, in most cases, extremely difficult to overturn a trial court's determination of fact—which is what your grade is. What you're asking your professor, essentially, is either to correct a clear error that they admit—or to throw yourself on the mercy of the court (the professor) for a few extra "mercy" points. (But keep in mind the constraints on the professor, not just ethical but also administrative.) What you're asking the *law school* to do is to throw out the trial court's determination and sub-

stitute their own judgment. Deans hate being asked to do this, and do it reluctantly (if at all). The standard for reversal is high—very high.

> At my school, a "gross violation of the instructor's own specified standards" is needed for the committee to change the grade.

This standard—a "gross violation" standard—is rarely met. Before you proceed you should be able to show that in fact there was a violation, and that it was not just any violation but a serious one, and that it wasn't just a violation of some concept of "fairness" but rather of a clear, specific statement of the professor's (most likely in the syllabus).

4. Weigh and weigh again the pros and cons of bringing a grade appeal. Additional matters to consider:

   a. The total picture. If you have one awful grade and five terrific grades, the picture is much better—and committees will be more likely to believe it—than if you have more than one potential grade appeal. In general, one grade appeal (while complicating things) is conceivable; more than that, no way.

   b. Time. If one of the schools you're applying to bases its decisions on rolling admissions, such as Harvard or Florida State, this can be quite pressing.

   c. Stress. An appeal is just what you need as you focus on your application, coursework, and doing well in both.

   d. Appearance. You'll need to submit addendums to notify and explain an appeal to transfer schools.

   e. Time II. It takes time to properly draft an effective appeal to your 1L school, explaining with detail and dispassion why a grade change is not just reasonable but required.

f. Consequences. If you are unable to transfer, how will you be viewed by your fellow students and professors? (As we all know, gossip really does spread fast—not just between students, but among professors as well.)

5. After weighing the pros and cons of your potential appeal, ask yourself one final time: "Do I really believe that a grade change is going to make a significant difference in an admissions committee's views of my application?" If the answer is "Yes", and you do not want any regrets, then move forward with the appeal but be prepared to deal with all that comes along with such action.

I found out that, amongst my peers, I was one of the few after Spring final exams to forget about everything that transpired during my first year of law school and attempt to enjoy my summer. Such a thought was short-lived. After the last exam, Property, I felt quite confident. I thought I had performed very well on the exams, and felt I had an excellent chance of transferring. Prior to the release of grades I was stress-free and taking in all I could of the sunshine and free time on my hands. Once grades began to trickle in, however, the tension began to escalate. I received 2 "A's" and 3 "A-minuses." I was still awaiting my final grade in Legal Writing when, a few days later, the infamous C+ posted. I felt as if the world around me was closing in. Just like that, I felt my chances of transferring to some of the top schools in the country dissipate in a matter of seconds. The time and effort I had put in to give myself a chance to attend a school that would change my life could potentially all be lost, all for one grade. I began to frantically call others in my class to see if the same fate had been visited upon them, some said "yes" and some answered "no." I began to forge a plan of action on how to handle this "stain" on my transcript.

I shuffled through the pages of my law school's Code of Conduct to learn how the grade appeal process worked. I had to first set up a meeting with my professor, and if unavailable, with the head of the department. I did, and after the meeting I was still not satisfied with the answers as to why I performed so poorly in the Legal Writing course. So, I began the grade appeal process outlined in the Code of Conduct.

I notified the schools I had applied to, with addenda, that I was appealing that grade, how I was handling the appeal, and the status of the appeal. I was extremely cautious not to come across as bashing my first-year school, or as a troublemaker who constantly contests decisions by faculty or the administration. This took careful thought and precise articulation: I did not want to hinder my chances of being accepted. Overcoming this obstacle in my pursuit to transfer was going to be difficult.

In the end, I lost my appeal and had to eat the "C+," but all was not lost as my goal to transfer to a top law school had become a reality. Who knows what decision may have been made as to my other applications had I won my appeal, elevating me to the top of my class. As we find out about the transfer (or any other) process, not all battles will be won—but you will not win a battle without putting up a fight, and the opportunities that come from battles won can change your life.

6

SUCCEEDING AT YOUR NEW SCHOOL AND BEYOND

Congratulations! You've gotten that fat envelope: the acceptance letter to the new law school of your dreams. You accept!

Your journey does not end, however. It is only just beginning anew. In addition to the many facets of getting used to a new school and new faces, there are important practical considerations, such as extracurricular opportunities and how to deal with "OCI," or the on-campus interview.

ON-CAMPUS-INTERVIEWS AS A TRANSFER

One of the first things you will do, besides the many housekeeping details such as finding a place to live, is to sign up for OCI. This does not quite get across just how important this is, however:

Overview and The Deadline. OCI is an acronym nearly everyone in law school has heard before. It is a process you should take advantage of. OCI is usually held a week or so before Fall classes start, and then the following couple weeks into the Fall semester. In OCI, employers from the area (or, if it's a national or quasi-national law school, from all over the country), travel to the law school to interview students for a potential 2L summer associate or summer clerk position. (In the national law schools, some employers will also hire for clerkships after the 1L year.)

First, contact your New 2L School *now*. Immediately. Make sure you can still participate in OCI. Most schools allow transfer students to participate in OCI, but with some schools getting their transfer offer admissions out to applicants late in the summer, transfer students can miss the OCI deadlines even if they are officially eligible to participate. Do not miss this deadline. Check the same day that you get your acceptance letter. Call your new school's Career Services or

Student Affairs offices and make sure you have not missed the deadline.

OCI can be somewhat of a jackpot lottery when finding a job, but it's definitely a process you want to take part in. One book that describes the OCI process and how to do well in these interviews is *The Insider's Guide to Getting a Big Firm Job*. It focuses on many of the subjective elements that can change a mere OCI invitation (based, in many cases, on the same factors that led to your transfer in the first place: grades) to an actual job at a great firm.

While employers—mostly the larger law firms—will be on campus to interview you and other students, the process starts weeks ahead, so even the "deadline" is really just that: the very tail end of an extended process. After that line is crossed, if you've not acted you're dead. That's why it is so important to contact your New 2L School *as soon as possible* about OCI.

The bidding for the law firms takes place in the late summer. One way to think of OCI is as a stampede. These are the jobs with the biggest firms, paying the highest salaries and with the biggest perks. Law students come a' running.

DON'T LET OCI AFFECT YOUR 2L TRANSITION

Much of what follows is more of the I-wish-someone-had-told-us-this-before variety. We learned the hard way.

Top grades at your Original 1L School and the leap to a higher-ranked school really *are* an accomplishment. Truth be told, many if not most students who transfer do so for better job opportunities. More specifically, for the chance to be courted rather than having to do the courting: OCI is exactly that, or at least it is as compared to students not invited to interview. The reason this is so vital is that firms will generally only travel to a limited number of law schools to interview. Nearly all firms will want a top student from a top law school. So, the higher you go, in terms of law school ranking, the more that is available in OCI. (And this is not a linear progression. A top law school might get ten times the number of firms interviewing than a school even a few dozen places lower in the rankings, and the firms interviewing will be different as well.) But you've made it into a higher-ranked law school, and so you hope to benefit from the greater career opportunities.

Well, here is your chance. OCI! This can make or break your summer job prospects if you want that "Big Law" summer job. While some students find summer law jobs on their own, usually with medium to smaller sized firms, the majority (as in 95 + %) of Big Law summer positions ("clerkships") go to law students through the OCI process.

Here is the warning however: Do not let OCI take over your first semester at your New 2L School. This is tricky, because OCI *is* important. But in addition to your reading, outlining, stress, and overall anxiety, you should also strive to fit into your new school.

So, our mantra for you: OCI is important, and you should participate actively, but do not let it distract you from your first semester at your New 2L School. We transfer students live in a different world than the rest of 2L law students; we are the exceptions to the rule. No, we are the exceptions *proving* the rule. The "rule" is the 2L who didn't have to transfer. For these students—the bulk of all law students, your 2L grades do not matter as much as your 1L grades. At times it seems that, for the "regular" 2L, grades are almost an afterthought: it's the 1L grades that make or break them.

It was 1L grades that made you. As a transfer student, however, employers want to see how you stack up against the student body at your New 2L School. So they're a bit more hesitant, and thus a bit more curious to make sure that we are as good in our New 2L School as we were in our Old 1L one. For us transfers, unlike for most 2Ls, our 2L grades are *still* important.

At one New 2L School, about one-quarter of the transfer students received summer clerkship offers from OCI. Given that the average 1L grades from successful transfer students is at or near the very top of their 1L classes, this is a lower percentage than a comparable group of 2L students from the 2L school. You should thus have a mindset that, while you will certainly seize any OCI opportunities, you might not receive a summer clerkship via OCI. You'll thus have to work a bit harder—as with the transfer itself.

If you do wind up getting an OCI offer, great. But, if not, you'll need to focus on grades and on finding your own post-2L job. This is why it's important to stay on track with your reading and outlining, and positioning yourself to receive the best 2L grades possible. You need, in essence, to take exactly the same approach in 2L as you did in 1L. Many 2Ls are not as serious in their second year, so this is the chance for you to shine in your new school as well. This will in turn maximize your chances of getting a summer position if you have to find a job on your own once OCI passes; your 2L grades are the first thing employers will look at. In sum, prepare yourself for OCI, take advantage of OCI, be serious about OCI, but keep your eye on the ball: your 2L grades.

With that by way of background, let's consider how some of the details of the OCI process affect the transfer student:

BIDDING

Once admitted to your New 2L School, you should receive information on how to access information on your new school's website or intraweb. Usually, there's a special site, or a restricted area of the main site, for students. Often it has a catchy name, so everyone at the school will know what such-and-so program means. At one school, the site is called "Symplicity." Whatever the name or variety of access at your school, be sure that you've not been inadvertently forgotten: even if the staff is apologetic for any oversight, they likely won't be able to correct any harm if you miss deadlines or simply aren't aware of that school's programs. You should thus ask the admissions office and career services office *as soon as you are accepted:* be sure that you know what's what.

Many law schools conduct the OCI process via their web-based program. Often, the programs work in very much a technical way: a student "bids" on an employer (either for an interview or for a chance for an interview), and only a certain number of interviews are actually granted.

Point #1: This is a competitive process. For most potential employers, there are more students who want to be interviewed than there are interview slots. Most firms conduct only a dozen or so interviews— as compared to hundreds who would be happy for the chance to work there. So, right from the start this is intensely competitive. Thus, you should bid assertively, and for many firms. Don't bid on firms you definitely wouldn't be interested in (which shouldn't be many), and do consider even opportunities you might not otherwise have thought of. At the very least, each interview is an opportunity to practice your interviewing skills.

Point #2: Be sure to include your transfer school in your résumé when applying for jobs for OCI. Yes, your profile will be a little odd as compared to the "average" 2L student, so you need to be especially careful to highlight your positive qualities while being clear about your 1L and 2L schools. Once you receive grades from your New 2L School you do not have to include your Original 1L School on your résumé. For OCI, you do—and will want to. Spotlight your terrific rank!

Point #3: Don't go into this process defensive about your 1L law school. After all, you did very, very well there. Keep a positive mindset, and chances are good that prospective employers will too.

Point #4: Pay attention. Each employer has its own expectations, both substantive (as to grades, etc.) and stylistic (what they want to see). You cannot treat each OCI employer as a "one size fits all" possibility. That's easier, of course, but it's not smart. Assess what each employer is asking for. Some employers ask for a résumé only, some ask for a résumé and transcript, some ask for a résumé, cover letter, and transcript. Some include information on who will be interviewing. (Of course, if that information is given, it's far better to personalize what you're submitting. It takes just minutes, and it can make the difference, especially with a borderline bid.) Further, tailor each bid to at least some detail specific to that employer. If they have a big labor law practice and you worked in a union, that's worth mentioning. (They might represent management rather than labor, but it will give them something unique to go on; chances are very good they would at least be curious—*i.e.,* more likely inclined to interview you.) If they're on Wall Street and you're worked in a brokerage firm, of course you want to mention that, probably in a cover letter as well as highlighted in your résumé. Don't stretch any fact too far, and be careful not to limit yourself: it's a fine balance, but you want to make yourself stand out (in a good way) to the hiring partners.

Point #5: Think about geography. Where do you want to practice? If you already know (and are certain of that choice), bid only on the firms from that locale. Don't take away someone else's interview if you're flat-out going to waste the interviewer's (and your own) time. If you do not have a specific city or area set in stone, bid on all the firms you can. You should cast your net as wide as possible: many employers prefer students who have grades from the school where the OCI is being done. After all, that's why they're there. While you have impressive grades, they are grades from your Original 1L School. Employers have a tough time comparing you to other students at your New 2L School because your grades came from a different law school with a different student body and most likely, a different grading curve. Being different—even if not perceived as "bad"—is still a negative. With many students to choose from, they might shy away from transfers. As mentioned, until you get your new grades at your New 2L School and prove yourself (again), there can be a stigma against transfers in the OCI process because of an assumption of a low LSAT score. Yes, not everyone who attends a Tier 4 law school has a below-par LSAT score; one may attend for a part time program or for personal reasons. That's the assumption, however, so it's best to understand and attempt to deal with it.

BIDDING: AN OVERVIEW

Each law school follows its own procedures, of course, but the LSAC has attempted to create a uniform approach. Thus, most law schools operate their OCI programs similarly.

With regard to your New 2L School, here's how it will likely work: a list of employers who have committed to coming to interview at your school is released. You click on the firms you want to bid on—*i.e.,* you send them your résumé and if possible a cover letter or even writing sample—and that's that. After a relatively short period (usually a few days), the bidding is closed.

The employer receives the résumés. They review and then submit to the school's Office of Career Services ("OCS") a list of students they wish to interview. At this point, you will know if you have been selected to interview with a firm, or if you are an alternate.

A few caveats: some schools require that employers interview some set percentage of students according to an open-bidding or random process, or sometimes according to that plus a cutoff. This will be explained in the OCS information, which you should find on the school's website (or by asking someone in the office). If the firm has not chosen to interview you but "has to" instead, it's of course more of a gamble—but most hiring partners operate on a "fresh start" principle of sorts: once you're in the interview room, everyone is assumed to be equally qualified. It's up to you to shine. (They *will* consider everything else when extending an offer, but in the interview—if you get one—you *do* have a chance. Don't think otherwise.)

The second quirk is that there are often "alternate" slots. If you're an alternate and a space opens up or someone declines their interview selection, you've got yourself an interview. This doesn't happen often, for obvious reasons, but that's no reason not to try. This anecdote is just another example of why your résumé needs to be top notch, and why you cannot assume anything in the OCI process. Your résumé is the "paper-you": while the OCI process can be somewhat arbitrary, and while there are clearly many variables in the hiring calculus, most firms make get their first impressions of you via your résumé.

I did not fare so well in OCI: 3 interviews with 20 bids, or a 15%. (Or, for baseball fans, at .150 I was batting below the Mendoza Line.) I did get interviews with two top-five national law firms. This is surprising now that I look back upon it. I was passed over for interviews with regional and local firms, but two top-five national firms with offices across the globe selected me for interviews. As my interview day approached, I got my suit pressed and was ready to go. I made packets for the interviewer. I checked the website, which stated I would be interviewed by a certain partner of the law firm. I checked his name, read his biography, and even read of his big cases in his bios. This is important to do as you want to be knowledgeable about your interviewer and be able to show him or her you did homework on their firm, their area of practice, and in particular about their background. So I went to my interview with two packets, one for the interviewer and one for me. The packets contained my résumé, transcript (from my 1L school), and writing sample. I printed out labels and personalized the folder for my interviewer as well. My packet contained notes about what I wanted to talk about and questions I wanted to ask about the firm. When I arrived for my interview, I was surprised to see two people already in the interview room. Faced with this awkward moment, of not having another packet for the second hiring partner at the interview, I handed my only prepared packet to one of the interviewers. To make a long story short, the other individual who came to the interview was the head hiring partner and I did not have a packet prepared for him. So as they shared the only packet I had prepared, not only did that significantly increase my already-high level of anxiety, I couldn't help but think of the advice I am about to give you: confirm how many people are scheduled to interview you, and prepare one extra packet just in case. If an extra interviewer is in the room, you're going to feel very, very good ... and so will they.

A CODE OF DRESS

You've heard it before: *Dress for Success!*

This is true, of course, when it comes to OCI interviews especially. We write "of course," but in reality this is not really an "of course." Some students simply do not understand just how important this is, or how it affects their chances in the interview room—which affects their chances with that firm, and in their career. Or even if they do understand, they don't act as if they do. The cause is irrelevant. The expectation is simple: you must dress well. You will not get "extra credit" for this, but you will be penalized—heavily—if you don't.

In an interview you are a law student who wants to be seen as a professional lawyer-in-being in the eyes of your interviewers. These hiring partners (and, often, a new associate) are very, very smart. They know that you are too. What they're looking for is not that you remember the prongs of such-and-so test. They want to know two things: can you act like a real-life lawyer, and will you fit in their firm? That's pretty much it. Everything you will talk about in the interview room will relate in some way to these two questions.

If you even think of taking a backpack into the interview room, you might as well skip it. Save yourself the time and stress of the interview: you will almost certainly not be asked back. Why? Because that is what a *student* carries. A *lawyer* brings an attaché case or portfolio, and knows how to handle it, shake hands, and engage in a reasonably fluid conversation.

Are you going to shave? (This applies to both men and women.) If not, skip the interview. It's a waste of your (and their) time. There aren't many practices where you can show up with a face (or legs) full of stubble. (And even if you want to be seen in the early morning with that been-slaving-away-here-all-night five-o'clock look, you had better have a shave kit in the office; you never know when the judge's clerk—or a senior partner—will call.)

Beards? No way. There are very, very few firms in which beards are seen. Even a moustache is almost as strong a no-no. Is this right? Wrong question. If you want even the hope of a job, you'd better learn how not to cause someone to wonder whether you will meet the second of the above two questions.

This isn't about "conformity"; it's about common sense. You need to show the *best* you in the interview. The best you is not the "unique" you. Now is not the time to "express yourself." You need instead to completely remove any thought about dress or hygiene in the minds of the interviewers. The best outcome is that they don't even think about this. The most they might say as they meet at the end of a very long day of a dozen-plus interviews is something like "Wow, this one looked sharp!"

CLOTHING. ONCE MORE.

Dress conservatively. This is not the time to try out that new magenta suit or bright yellow shirt with a top hat to match (no senior prom canes either). No bow ties. No cummerbunds. In fact, nothing that's even the tiniest bit unusual in a real-world office.

That's why we're making such a big deal of this. Because students are around, well, other students most of the time, it's easy to forget just what the law degree leads to. A lot of larger firms are full-service business firms. Their clientele are paying the bills, and are demanding. If a partner even gets a whiff that you'll cause embarrassment to the firm (and to them), there's not a chance you'll be invited into their conference room. (And you'll probably not even get the invite to the front door.) The bottom line of law firms—and of most law offices? This is all still driven by clients. Thus, senior partners are *very* concerned about every aspect of what goes before clients and the community, and the first question—can you learn to act like a lawyer—is very much relevant.

To get that interview, you absolutely must be seen as a peer professional. You want to create an image so that they say, consciously or sub-consciously, "That person reminds me of a sharp lawyer already at the firm." Thus, stick to dark suits, a conservative (and well-pressed) dress shirt, and a non-eccentric tie. Cufflinks and a watch are always a plus—as long as you feel comfortable wearing them. Leave the sneakers at home.

[Editor's note: we almost deleted several of these passages, but decided not to: you would be amazed at the stories hiring partners tell of what students do to kill their own chances at an interview. Bad dress is near the top of the list.]

WHAT TO BRING?

Confirm what the firm has asked you to bring to the interview. Obviously you need to bring a résumé—a perfect copy—and you absolutely need to bring extras. These should be in a professional folder or binder. "Professional" means thin, and clean. You do not want to bring in some bulky old briefcase, or some torn-up old briefcase. If you don't have one, or cannot afford one, see if you can borrow one, or ask for one for your birthday.

If you make packets, as recommended above, be sure to bring an extra.

If anything could conceivably go wrong, try to have a replacement or extra. In addition to making you look super-prepared (and thus worthy of hiring), it might help ease your mind a bit.

CHOOSING THE INTERVIEW TIME SLOT

If you are chosen to be interviewed, you will usually find out via your school's website. You'll then select an interview time slot.

There are only so many interview time slots allocated, so check online often (as in several times a day, or immediately if you know when the time slots post), and select your time. Signing up early is especially important because you do not want your interview time slot to conflict with a class—even if sometimes it feels great to excuse yourself from class in your snappy suit, on your way to obvious success.

This might not seem like such a big deal, but remember: as a transfer 2L your grades still matter. The last thing you want to do is fall behind in your classes because of OCI. If you are forced to interrupt class time, you should still go to the class, and when it is time for you to leave, do so quietly. Position yourself near the door and don't have all of your papers out: just a simple notepad should be sufficient. As courtesy, be sure to notify the professor before class that you'll need to excuse yourself, and the reason why. Few will object, and this is one of those professional courtesies that can help with building professional relationships with your new professors— and is a good habit to get into.

Once you have selected your interview time slot, you're now committed. *Do not miss your interview!* As you can imagine, this is seen as unprofessional—and even more so, you might get into hot water with the OCS office and administration of your New 2L School.

A student missed an OCI interview he had scheduled. He was asked to write a letter of apology to the firm and to the Dean of the law school. That is not how you want to start off your new 2L year at your new law school.

Remember, this is the school you will graduate from; networking and reputations are *very* important now. Especially if you attend a higher-ranked school, the student sitting next to you might one day be a hiring partner at a big law firm, a future judge, or a future Senator.

INTERVIEWING: AFTER THE INTERVIEW

The interviewers will meet immediately after the interview. Think about this: you are tired after one interview. Imagine how tired they are after one or two dozen! There they sit, after a day in a small, windowless, stale room—trying to recall the individuals they've met in rapid succession. Truth be told, they're lucky to remember half of them. That's right. After all that stress, they might not even remember having spoken with you.

Here's where this can be important to you: interviewers generally put candidates into three piles: the definite *Yes'es,* the definite *No's,* and the middle *Maybe's.* They might have just a few candidates who really stand out. How? These are the candidates who are sharp, who look sharp, and who come across as true professionals: personable, confident, mature. Not forced, not timid, not overbearing. The ones who stand out in a negative way are easy: they are forced, or timid, or overbearing. These two piles are relatively easy to sort. They'll probably agree on the one or two clear *Yes'es,* they'll almost certainly agree on the half-dozen *No's,* and they'll discuss the rest. Chances are, a single negative thought will doom anyone in this group. The negative will come from any of the above criteria. They'll likely have just a handful of open positions, so they're probably going to be discussing just a small handful of the *Maybe's,* if any.

Part of why this is important is for the next stage: if they put someone who is unlikely to shine in the call-back interview, not only have they wasted time (and a lot of money), but they will embarrass themselves to their colleagues. They don't want to embarrass themselves to their colleagues. So, make their job easier. You want to show not only that you are all of those good qualities; you want to show that everyone else will see those good qualities too.

INTERVIEWING: ADDITIONAL CONCERNS

Here's a cardinal mistake made in the OCI process:

> I am from [choose any area of the country of interest to you], and knew I wanted to return to that area to practice upon graduation
>
>> For my OCI, about half of the firms were from that area, but the other half were from other parts of the state, and some were

from out-of-state as well. Not wanting to practice anywhere else, I bid only for the firms from my preferred locale.

This was my first mistake. Being a transfer student especially, I could have increased my chances of landing an OCI job. I should have bid on firms in other areas of the state, and possibly even in other cities that seemed to be quite attractive. My exclusionary tactic greatly restricted my options, in a process that is already quite limited.

Furthermore, being head-strong about getting a Big Law summer associate position, I did not bid on smaller firms. This was an even bigger mistake. I not only excluded about half of the firms because of location, I then excluded *another* half of the firms that were left because of my fascination with a Big Law job. Statistically, I had cut down my pool of potential employers by seventy-five percent!

Additionally, being a transfer student, I should have considered that my chances were *much* better with smaller and mid-sized firms, where the competition is less fierce. Not only that, but some smaller firms *do* have cachet in their area: these can be "spin offs" with partners from the largest firms. You should not treat all firms as alike based on mere data. There's much more to firms than that.

In all, I bid on approximately 20 firms. I received 3 interviews—all from very large and prestigious law firms—but by not bidding on other, smaller firms, I severely limited myself and my options.

Bottom line: If you do not care about location, blanket your bidding on as many firms as possible. If your school sets a maximum, be strategic about where and to whom you bid, but don't count any firm out based on any simplistic measure. Also, don't limit yourself to a particular firm within a particular practice field. If you absolutely know you want to do corporate law, then of course you should not bid on firms that do litigation. But, if you are not sure, do not limit yourself. There are other fields of law you may not have experienced yet, and you might just find that you enjoy it.

THE INEVITABLE QUESTION

"So, why did you transfer?"

This question is bound to come up. You may not get it in every interview. (But you probably will.) At some point, as the interview progresses, you will hear the words: "So, Ms. Jones, I see here that you started at [a glance down] ABC Law School. Interesting. Why did you decide to transfer to the XYZ School of Law?"

This is one of those loaded questions, where the questioner is looking as much for how well you react as for the actual answer. (Remember an adage in trial practice: never ask a question you don't already know the answer to.) You absolutely must be ready for it.

As you sit there and try to think of non-vocational reasons, such as, "Well my family lives here," or, "I like the nationally known environmental law program," just be honest. If those are the real reasons you transferred, fine. But don't try to hide behind the career opportunities. After all, part of being in a firm is being very much aware of how law practice *is* a career, a real-world profession. You need to convey that you know that too.

This is not the admissions committee. (You're already in!) This is world of the practice- and practical-oriented, high-powered law firm attorney. They know the score.

The interviewer knows why you transferred: to go to a higher-ranked law school and improve your job prospects with firms such as theirs, which almost certainly would not have granted you the interview at your original school. For whatever reason you went to your original T3 or T4 law school, the fact is a substantial portion of us attend a lower-ranked law school because of our LSAT score. Don't be ashamed. Many, many potential law students never even get the chance to go to law school, and the bottom line is that you did well—very well—in your 1L year, and you wanted to capitalize on that. There's nothing wrong with that, and nearly every interviewer would agree.

Just be honest; the interviewer knows why you transferred—for a better job. Chances are they admire you for it ... but they must still confirm your qualities for their firm.

Accordingly, if you made a lateral transfer and your reasons were personal, explain that. Interviewers want to know why you are now attending your 2L law school, and they want to know if you will be in that area when you graduate and beyond. So, relocating to be with family will be a plus—at least a modest one. The last thing a firm wants to do is offer a summer associate job to someone who will not be in that area—or who *might* not be in that area—or who just seems a little bit flaky. This goes to the issue of "maturity," so if this is a plus for you, it's a plus.

Hiring partners will ask you background information and delve into your past for clues about the future: whether or not you are likely to be a good associate who *wants* to stay with them, and thus whether or not you will waste their time and money now. They are keenly interested in clues as to why you should be with *that* firm. Your answers and follow-up questions should therefore be directed to addressing those concerns.

THANK YOU LETTERS AND FOLLOW-UP

After your interview, it is time to write the thank you letter. This letter is another part of the interviewing process, and should be seen as exactly that.

It is common courtesy to thank the interviewer for his or her time at the end of the interview, of course, but that is not enough. You should also thank them in a formal thank you letter. Your letter should be not only formal, it should be personal. Yes, this seems like something your grandmother talked about when you were a kid. No matter. This is part of professional good manners, and it does make a difference.

In your letter, you should reinforce what it was that connected in the interview. This is a great opportunity to re-emphasize your qualities, and to connect those qualities with the topics the interviewers discussed. If they focused on a certain practice area or project, now's a great time to mention your interest in just such an area or project (assuming, of course, that that's true). You can also thank them for conversational tidbits, such as a common link mentioned in the interview.

This should be specific, as much as possible. It's not a long note, but it should mention some detail of interest to the interviewer and to the firm. You can close by highlighting why you are an ideal fit for the firm, and would very much like to meet with them further to discuss your qualities, etc. If they are an entertainment firm and you played NCAA collegiate athletics, you can bring that up in your thank you letter. If the firm is a business litigation firm and you have an MBA, you can bring that up. In sum, show *that* firm why you are their ideal candidate.

You can take another opportunity to highlight an accomplishment—or perhaps a strong point you forgot to mention in the interview. You can, implicitly, show them those strong points, as well as a caring and detail-oriented personality.

In short, the thank you letter is a fantastic opportunity to "close the deal"—at least to get your foot in the firm's door (literally) with the call-back interviews. Do not just be another name on a piece of paper with boilerplate lingo that shows you did not even bother to take the time to personalize your letter to the interviewers and their firm.

You want the interviewer to receive your thank you letter as soon as possible after the interview—ideally the day after they get back to the office. So, send the thank you letter *immediately* after the interview is over. This might sound like logical advice and something you would normally do anyway, but you'd be surprised at how often this *doesn't* happen. It's also easy to treat this as a superfluous, even silly tradition that doesn't really matter. To show that the opposite is true I'll offer one example: my own.

In addition to OCI, I sent my résumé and cover letters to larger firms in the area, hoping to for an interview. One firm wrote back. In response to my cover letter, the hiring partner said he would be willing to meet with me on a Friday a few weeks hence. After some back-and-forth emails, we arranged a time to meet for lunch for an interview.

Wanting the hiring partner to receive my thank you letter around the forty-eight hour mark after our interview, or the following Monday, I mailed out the thank you letter the Friday morning of my interview. Well, as luck would have it, I got an email from the hiring partner that morning saying that something came up and he would have to reschedule my interview for sometime the following week.

Well, with the letter already in the mail you can guess what happened. The letter would arrive at the firm's office on Monday, and I was supposed to have had my interview the Friday before. Oops.

I called the hiring partner's secretary (embarrassing) and explained the situation (very embarrassing), and she kindly offered to hold onto the letter until after my interview. While things worked out, it was an unnecessary and easily avoidable predicament: had I waited to mail the letter until *after* my interview was over. Not only that, but I realized after the interview that I could have written a much better letter had I waited. I won't ever make that mistake again.

HITTING THE WALL: OR, WHAT TO DO WHEN OCI FAILS YOU

One word (well actually two words): Mail Merge!

If you strike out in OCI—as many do—it is still possible to find a great summer job. The trick, of course, is that you must do so on your own. While you have to put in some additional work to find the firms and make the contacts, there are ways to make your work streamlined, so you work smarter rather than harder.

First, assess yourself. Take a realistic look at your qualifications. Second, take a look at who you're going after. Nearly all big law firms fill their summer positions—all of their summer positions—through OCI. In fact, as you learned in OCI, there are many, many students eager to take those jobs. So, it's not for a lack of supply that any job goes unfilled. Thus, if you send a thousand letters to every big law firm in the United States, you are almost certainly wasting dozens of hours of effort, lots of postage, two reams of high-quality and expensive letterhead, and two boxes of equally high-quality and even more expensive envelopes. We'll not get into how much licking of those envelopes will also be wasted.

Instead of beating your head against the wall, try something else instead: think about what type of law you *really* want to practice, and focus your search in that area. If you don't have a genuine preference as to the type of law you wish to practice, but do know a geographical area, that's fine too. If you know neither the type nor geographic area, that also is fine: chances are you can focus your solicitations in nearby offices, which will save expense and trouble—and give a greater chances of interviews—for the summer. And even if none of that works, all is not lost.

To start from scratch, take the above factors. If you have a serious interest in a specific field and some clear reasoning behind that (say, an interest in environmental law and a master's degree in geology), you can refine a list of potential firms by practice area. This will almost certainly be more useful to you than the more generic approach of most firms in OCI. You then build a mailing list of those firms' hiring partners with a carefully drafted letter than seeks a summer job. You follow up each of those letters with an email or phone call, perhaps one week to ten days after the letter is received. Chances are good you'll get at least some interest, especially if your qualifications are closely aligned with that firm's practice.

If you don't have a preference as to the type of law you wish to practice but do know a geographical area, you'll go through the same process, but will instead focus on mid-sized and smaller firms in your target area. You'll need to be even more careful in your letter, as you want to come across as a sincere potential associate.

You might also investigate governmental and non-profit possibilities, or even openings with a court or judge. Depending upon your long-term plans, in many cases it is the exposure to the workings of a law office—rather than the actual office itself—that future employers are most concerned about. They want to see that you know what you're getting into—and a glowing reference from a senior colleague is extremely helpful.

What if you really, truly want to practice in a big firm? All is still not lost. If your qualifications are top-notch (good 2L grades from a T14 school or super-good grades from a T1 or T2 school, for example), you can build your list with firms that did not recruit at your school's OCI. You might need to travel to the first interview, but why not? That's a fair shot at a good job. Most firms hire almost exclusively from their OCI schools, but if your qualifications, connection, and presentation are sufficiently sparkling, they might give you a shot. While still a long shot, that's not the waste that a blind mass-mailing would be.

Two websites are invaluable in researching prospective employers. To target Big Law firms that did not participated in your New 2L School's OCI process, use the NALP Directory of Legal Employers (www.nalpdirectory.com). This website offers searchable, detailed information about firms, including summer associate statistics, and, most importantly, contact information for the firm's hiring partner or administrator. Address your correspondence accordingly. The downside to the NALP site is that mostly larger firms are on it. If you want to research medium or smaller sized firms, as you should, use Martindale Hubbell (www.martindale.com).

From there, you should use Microsoft Word's Mail Merge feature and Microsoft Excel to create your letter template and database. Mail Merge allows you to import data from Microsoft Excel so you can personalize letters to law firms in an expeditious fashion. The process is quite simple. In Microsoft Excel, create columns for each firm's pertinent information, such as the first and last name of the hiring partner, the firm's name, the address, etc. (You can also do this directly in Word.) If you're not familiar with this, get a book from the library or follow the Mail Merge Wizard; this function is a huge time-saver, allowing you to create dozens of letters in about as much time as it takes to do one.

OTHER WAYS TO NETWORK

You've no doubt heard the saying, "It's not what you know, it's who you know." While clichéd, to a large extent this is true. As a transfer student, you do not have any grades at your new school, and the OCI process can be difficult for anyone. There are still other avenues to pursue for jobs, however.

First, check with your school's Office of Career Services or the Office of Student Affairs. These generally offer general information on firms that do not use OCI, but which might still be interested in hiring for summer or part-time positions.

I knew of a transfer student who stopped by the Office of Career Services and noticed a posting about a summer associate position with a local law firm. The firm had missed our fall OCI, and had contacted the Office of Career Services. He was one of the first students to contact the firm, and wound up getting the summer associate position.

While this might be part luck, this brings to mind the adage about "luck being what happens when preparation meets opportunity." There's lots of opportunity out there, in any legal community. The more prepared you are, the more likely a firm will snap you up!

Additionally, often through social functions, OCS offers opportunities to network with local lawyers and judges. If you belong to an organization or club in law school, or even if you are not a member, many organizations routinely organize functions where alumni and judges attend. You can also join local bar associations, or attend as a student member (often at reduced cost or for free), and gain valuable contact in a professional setting—no one will mind that you're a student, and in fact most will appreciate your initiative. As a transfer student, it is important to put yourself out there and network with as many peers, lawyers, and judicial officials as possible.

Another way to network is to work or volunteer part-time with an agency or firm. While it is difficult to fit in additional duties outside of law school, pro bono or volunteer activities can be *very* rewarding. First, law school is classroom-driven. Besides the occasional externship or clinic, most of what we learn in law school is within the confines of a classroom. Volunteering allows you to get out of the classroom and get hands-on experience with real lawyers and real clients.

Where to volunteer? Well, that depends on your personal interests and career goals. Ideally, you would strive to volunteer with a firm or agency in the practice area you're interested in. This not only allows you to get your foot in the door with that firm or agency (and thus other firms), it opens up the possibility of a job offer when you graduate. It also provides real-world experience, and the possibility of a mentor and future referrer. Private firms are less likely to take on volunteers than other public agencies. (Firms are more likely to have—or create—part-time positions than unpaid ones.) Public agencies such as the Legal Aid Society, the State Attorney's Office, the Public Defender's Office, or programs such as Guardian ad Litem are usually more willing to take on volunteers.

Additionally, if you plan on going into litigation, these options are ideal: potential employers will be impressed with experience in any of these offices. In fact, even if you want to be a prosecutor, for example, but the local DA's office doesn't have a volunteer program, a stint in a Legal Aid office will still count: it gives you the other side of the criminal procedure picture. Or, if you know you want to be a corporate lawyer, volunteering a state agency will provide you a real-world experience—and a real-world reference—in return for your time. If that wasn't enough to sell you on the positives of volunteering, many law schools award Pro Bono Certificates upon graduation to law students who accumulate a certain number of pro bono hours. Some law schools have levels of Pro Bono accomplishment: thirty-five hours of volunteer service for a General Pro Bono Certificate; seventy-five hours for an Excellence Certificate; and a whopping one hundred and five hours gets you an Outstanding Achievement Certificate.

Another way to network is through what we'll call the "Lawyers Secret Society": The Inns of Court (www.innsofcourt.org), a social-networking organization run across the country by law students, lawyers, and judges. Each Inn of Court usually organizes functions once a month for its members to discuss pertinent legal and ethical topics in the community. This is another chance for you to break bread with local attorneys and judges while increasing your knowledge of (and thus ability to discuss) current legal and ethical issues.

Another option is to contact Student Services and inquire about contacting previous transfer students who transferred into your New 2L School. Remember, they too had to go through the same process as you arc going through now, and might be willing and able to provide you with an excellent resource or even a potential job opportunity. Like yourself, a transfer alumni had to bust their proverbial butt, just like you, and can empathize with your situation.

In sum, do not bank on OCI to land you a job. For us transfers, even in our new schools, it's not always this easy. So be prepared to do the extra work (this should be nothing new) to put yourself in the best possible position for that perfect job. The worst that can happen? You put in a little extra work, get a lot of extra contacts, and manage to also land a job through OCI. That's what we'll call a good problem.

A BIG FIRM VIEW

Here is a view from a partner at a national law firm on the recruitment process generally, and on interviewing specifically. As it's often better to hear directly from those who actually do the interviewing and hiring, this might help reinforce many of the above points:

Firms care a lot about what law school you graduate from. They care a lot less what law school you started with.

The bottom line is that we expect to be providing almost 100% on-the-job training. We do not place a lot of value on practical skills you learn in class in law school. Instead, we look at your law school (and, indeed, at your entire résumé) as a proxy for intelligence, work ethic, and other good things we value but which cannot be taught.

Getting into a top law school is difficult. If you got into a top law school, therefore, that law school determined that you are special, and we will piggyback on that determination. It doesn't really matter whether that determination happened after college or after a year at another law school. If *Great Law School* blessed you, that's all I need to know (as far as blessings go). You pass the initial quality test just like every other *Great Law School* student. Just like class rank, GPA, and course selection, law school ranking/reputation is a tool for determining your capabilities ahead of the interview.

We will probably ask you about your school transfer, but perhaps as much for general conversation as anything else. We're not trying to put you on the spot—we wouldn't have invited you if we weren't sufficiently impressed—so there's no need to get defensive. (That, in fact, is a red flag for us. It's important that you're comfortable in your own skin.) If you transferred from, say, the University of Illinois to Yale (as did one of my classmates), it is pretty obvious why you transferred. No one dislikes Illinois—but Yale tells us something special. Most transfers are "up" to a better school, and the presumption is that you are simply upgrading your school. If it's error at all, it's a harmless one. If the transfer is not to an obviously better school, then there might be more questions, but otherwise the discussion will mostly be social: "So, how do you like New Haven compared to Champaign?"

Transferring to a better law school tells us three things about you: (1) you didn't get into the better school on your first try; (2) you did well enough during your first year to get into the better school on your second try; and (3) you made the effort to actually apply and transfer to the better school while doing well as a 1L.

Of those three things, only the first is a negative. The other two are strong positives, and number three in particular will count in your favor as it demonstrates maturity and determination. So it will behoove you to subtly direct the emphasis towards that third point and away from your not-quite-good-enough LSAT/undergraduate GPA. Even if your college résumé is not so impressive, you want to remind us that, in the end, you were blessed by a good law school and that you went out of your way and worked hard to get that blessing.

One of the things we look for when interviewing (or reviewing résumés) is a candidate who has accomplished something difficult—particularly something difficult that required hard work and dedication. When we interview an Olympic athlete we are automatically interested—not because we have a need for speedskaters, but because we know that rising to that level of athletic achievement requires immense (and intense) dedication and hard work, and dedication and hard work are the things we do need. They're thus the things we look for.

And while transferring law schools isn't exactly an Olympic competition, it falls into the same category. While everyone else was just trying to survive their 1L year, you were excelling in your first year, restarting the application process anew, and working hard to keep your grades up to impress the new school. That shows a lack of complacency with your current situation and a determination to better yourself—both traits we like.

As for the many other details of interviewing, frankly, they don't matter as much. The main goal, to put not too fine a point on it, is not to shoot yourself in the foot. Send a post-interview note. No one is impressed by your note, most won't even read your note, and most won't care…but some do get offended or at least notice it if you don't send a note. So send a note. Your writing sample should not be bad. Free of errors, full of logic and consistent thought. Whether it is a letter or a brief is not so important, and we are not looking for the ultimate legal argument ever written. We just want a writing sample that shows that you can write something non-bad. You will not get hired because of your awesome writing sample, but you will get dinged (and thus likely rejected) because of a bad writing sample.

In general, much of interviewing is simply not screwing it up. There are a few areas where you will be judged on a qualitative scale—academics, intelligence, social skills, personality—but there are many more that are just pass/fail: writing sample, attire, general appearance, timeliness, etc. Don't waste time and money buying an expensive designer suit—just don't blow it by not wearing a suit at all. Don't fret all night with the precise wording of your first twelve sentences. Relax. Fret a little bit, sure, but don't let your nervousness consume your good traits. Just come across as a decent, earnest future associate, and perhaps you'll get your chance with that firm to be one.

And don't worry about your status as a transfer law student. Look instead to impress interviewers with the qualities that led you to transfer in the first place. What you've done is a worthy accomplishment—after all, you probably wouldn't have gotten the interview at all had you remained at your original law school—so be confident, and show us those good qualities.

While we would love to give you the name of this contributor, he requested anonymity lest any statement or inference come back to haunt him or his firm. We can state that he is a partner in a national firm, and has been involved in the hiring process for many years.

7

To Your Success

Congratulations! You have done very, very well in your 1L law school, you've jumped through all the hoops and have successfully transferred to your new 2L law school, you've navigated all of the social and practical obstacles, and you've landed a great position, which will lead to a fantastic and rewarding career.

This has not been easy. We know. But transferring law schools speaks to your character and ultimate success: the challenges you overcome, and the successes you will enjoy … each of these is testament to your abilities and motivation to accomplish more than you otherwise would.

In this, we lift our glasses in a toast to your success, and we encourage you to share your stories with others. Please visit our publisher's website (www.fineprintpress.com) to send us a note about what we might have explained more fully, or topics we forgot to include, or just personal narratives that will add to future students' awareness when transferring. Please also take a moment to consider just how valuable your efforts are. It is in the achieving of what one wants—sometimes "against all odds"—that we truly appreciate what it is we gain. As challenging as the process sometimes is, we guarantee that it will be worth it.

We wish you the very best, and congratulate you in your future success.

Epilogue: A Concluding View

We have spent much of this book highlighting dangers in the transfer process—as well as problems that, with foresight and preparation, can be avoided.

Here is a narrative from a student who successfully transferred and who suffered from many of the same issues we recount. We hope his view reinforces ours in encouraging you to guard against these pitfalls. We also hope this serves as an encouragement to you—to contemplate and to complete your transfer application.

Here is his story:

I don't regret my transfer. I deeply regret my transfer.

No, this is not the symptom of a mental illness for which I should seek treatment and/or disclose on my bar application. Given a second chance, I would definitely transfer again, but I would also work to change many of the repercussions of my transfer.

The decision to transfer was not difficult. In December of my 1L year, my girlfriend and I decided to get married. I lived in Cincinnati; she lived in Indianapolis. Neither wanted a long-distance relationship for my remaining two years of law school. She had recently built a house; I was living with my mother. There was thus little debate: I was coming to her.

As I finished my 1L year at Cincinnati, I heard classmates talking about on-campus interviewing. From what I picked up, the top law firms would hire the top law students as "summer associates," and ridiculously overpay them for three months of non-work. It sounded like a great gig, but the goal for the firm was to identify those law students they wished to eventually hire as associates. I was in the top 10% of my class—prime material for OCI—but I brushed it off. I was about to leave Cincinnati and not look back, and so being truthful about my plans and obtaining one of these lucrative summer associate positions seemed mutually exclusive. I was stupid and in love, so I felt I could afford to ignore OCI. (I am still one of these attributes; which of the two is left as an exercise for the reader and/or my wife.)

The transfer process itself was relatively straightforward: I collected transcripts, wrote a quick one-page essay on why I was transferring (basic thesis: I'd rather live with my wife than my mother), and enclosed a check for a few hundred dollars for the seat deposit. Indiana University at Indianapolis was slightly lower on the *U.S. News and World Report* totem pole than the University of Cincinnati, and my grades were stellar, so I had no worries about being accepted. I also submitted a one-page letter to the IU-Indy Office of Financial Aid, requesting that I be considered for in-state tuition. I had secured one year of full-time work as a law clerk in Indianapolis, and that year away from school would secure my status as an Indiana resident for tuition purposes. I was accepted, and my seat deposit was ultimately returned to me. The law school decided to waive the deposit because I was a transfer student.

I took seriously my year away from law school, making marriage my number one priority. I tuned out most thoughts or worries about job hunting. I did contact one of the professors at my new law school. (I had begun talking with him shortly after I became engaged and knew I would transfer. I wanted to hit the ground running in my area of passion, copyright law.) I also met with the Dean of Students to compare my Cincinnati 1L curriculum with the 1L curriculum at IU-Indy. I would have to take two more credit hours of torts and two more credit hours of contracts, but I received (at the least) elective credit for all of my 1L courses.

When it came time to register for classes, I discovered that I was unable to do so. After much frustration using the school's website, and after several phone calls, I discovered the cause of this problem: while my future classmates worked en masse to occupy seats in courses I had all-but-assumed I'd be taking, I had never been flagged as an admitted student. My guess is that cashing the seat deposit is the internal step when the law school "flips the switch" on an applicant, changing them to an "admitted student" in the relevant databases. When the law school returned my seat deposit (rather than apply it towards tuition, as seat deposits generally are), I surmise that I was never marked as admitted, and thus could not register. As a consequence, I was blocked out of my first-choice courses. *Arghh!* (Thankfully, I was able to work in these courses before graduation.)

When I arrived at the law school in August to buy books before classes started, I stopped by the Office of Professional Development. I inquired about OCI and how to get started. The staff informed me that the deadline to sign up had already passed. My wife's dream of her husband being vastly overpaid for a summer of non-work was dashed. (I don't begrudge her that dream; after all, it's been her salary that's supported us the last three years.)

Not surprisingly, this turn of events was as unexpected as it was unwelcome. I was not a happy new 2L. I contacted every major firm in Indianapolis, explaining why the deadline had been missed, and requesting that I be considered for their OCI. I netted one interview, which did not lead to a callback. Missing OCI was a blow, but the magnitude of the loss did not become apparent until the Great Recession picked up steam in the late summer of 2008. No firms interviewed me the following year, as 3Ls were routinely ignored. Firms were retrenching as it was; they had little interest in bringing on additional weight, no matter how highly qualified. (By then, I was 4th in my class, had won Moot Court, and had interned with a federal judge.)

Another mistake I made during transfer was not pursuing a place on the school's flagship law review, the *Indiana Law Review*. In contrast to OCI, this was a product of conscious choice, and not simply being uninformed of the process or deadline. I had made a choice to focus my time on outside projects that would impress technology-focused employers such as Google, rather than jumping through the traditional hoops that law firms looked for. (My goals have since changed, and so on further examination the "traditional hoops" don't look quite so bad.) I chose to focus on working directly with my copyrights professor and on the *Life of a Law Student* website. I'll also admit being turned off by having to "write on" to the law review. Although the top 10% of the 1L class was automatically invited without the need to go through a writing competition, my top 10% 1L status (at a higher-ranked law school, no less) did not count at my 2L law school.

So, in my transfer, OCI and law review were my two mistakes. But not everything could go wrong, could it? I did make some smart decisions. Marrying my wife is at the top of that list. She's promised that even if I put my law degree to use bagging groceries, she will still love and stay with me.

Other than Laura, touching base with my copyright professor at my new school was perhaps my best move. I knew that I wanted to study and practice in this area, which he taught. He and I developed a rapport, based in our common interest, and having a mentor and friend on the faculty was especially important for me. Tenured faculty teach 1L courses, and because I had not taken 1L courses at IU-Indy, I did not know and have relationships with as many faculty. Also, by coming in as a married transfer student, I did not know anyone from a shared 1L section and my meager social time was generally spent with my wife. My relationship with this professor helped me to feel that I was not completely alone.

I made a conscious effort to establish relationships with other professors as well. I enjoyed my Trusts and Estates course, and when I learned that the professor would also be teaching Family Law the next semester—a course helpful for the Bar Exam—I made it a priority to take that class as well. My grade in her class and well-timed book recommendation (she ended up loving Jeffrey Toobin's *The Nine* as much as I did), allowed me to rely upon her for a third letter of reference when it came time to apply for judicial clerkships.

So what are my recommendations for transfer students?

> **First,** find out how your transfer school handles OCI. Stop reading right now, and call them. Find out *before the deadline* how to get signed up for OCI. Go ahead. Put down this book. Call the OCI office of your transfer school(s) right now. I'll wait.
>
> Welcome back. Aren't you glad you got that cleared up now, before you potentially ruined your entire law career by getting left out of the summer associate programs?

> **Second,** find out if you can qualify for in-state tuition. Obviously, this is a moot point if you are transferring to a private school. However, you can save tens of thousands of dollars if you are going the public school route. Each state has its own standard. Indiana's test, for example, is physical presence in the state for one year with a predominate purpose other than education. Find out the test, and what

office you need to appeal to in order to obtain in-state tuition.

Third, touch base with at least one professor in a subject you care about. Explain that you are planning (or at least considering) transferring to their law school, you are interested in their field, and would like to get their thoughts. Offer to take them out to get coffee when you are in town. If you are knowledgeable about their field, don't be afraid. Asking intelligent questions about their area of expertise is a great way to establish rapport and begin a relationship. If you aren't knowledgeable (besides knowing you want to study in that area), pull up the articles written by this professor, and read them. Simply being able to discuss their work—as nonchalantly as possible—will go far. Professors, like most human beings, love it when people willingly read their work. Independently familiarizing yourself with their scholarship also demonstrates initiative and drive, which most law professors respect out of students especially.

Fourth, suck it up. Apply for law review even if a write-on competition is involved (as it almost certainly is). Thankfully, I was able to join one of my school's other law reviews, and was still able to write an article (a student "Note") about copyright law. Fair or not, however, there is a prestige drop between the flagship law review and other journals at a law school. Also, if you end up on a non-flagship journal, you will be restricted on the subject matter you can write on for your note. (Flagship law reviews generally cover all subjects, while other journals focus on specific legal areas.) I joined the *Indiana International & Comparative Law Review,* and was able to analyze the interaction between various domestic sources of law and a semi-obscure provision of the leading copyright treaty. I ultimately had to write-on to the *II&CLR,* so I should have simply bit the bullet and tossed my hat into the ring, to mix metaphors, for all three reviews the year before. Finally, although the flagship review ostensibly considered incoming

3Ls for a one-year term, few ever succeeded. (None were offered during my 3L year.)

In summary, I am very happy about my transfer. Except for the parts that I am very unhappy about. But since you've had the foresight to read this book, you can (hopefully) avoid these and other pitfalls.

Good luck!

Neil Wehneman earned a bachelor's degree in Information Systems from the Fisher College of Business at The Ohio State University. He spent his first year of law school at the University of Cincinnati College of Law, where he finished in the top 10% of his class while recording the Life of a Law Student podcast. He subsequently transferred to the Indiana University School of Law at Indianapolis, where he graduated summa cum laude.

APPENDIX A:
SAMPLE TRANSFER STATEMENT

Here is a sample transfer statement, which was part of a successful application to a top law school:

Applying to transfer to Ocean Law School is a long-awaited dream come true. Looking to the intellectual, innovative, and prestigious programs at both Ocean University and its Law School, I have envisioned myself amid its students and future leaders for many years. It is the school that I dreamed of attending for my undergraduate studies. Due to a lack of financial resources, however, I recognized that I did not have the funds to attend Ocean University during undergraduate and graduate school. I thus attended West Pond College. Keeping my dream alive, however, I challenged myself to excel, and was awarded a scholarship and later gained admission to the West Bay Graduate School.

I attended West Lagoon College of Law, where I benefitted greatly from a full scholarship. During my first year of law school, which is among the most intense year of study for anyone, I achieved a ranking among the top students, by grades, among a group of 199 fellow students. This is a great honor, of course, but equally important are the many friends among these students. Still, a dream beckons: to attend and graduate from Ocean Law School.

I am especially interested in Ocean Law School's programs in international and comparative business law. I am at a serious disadvantage at West Lagoon College of Law because I wish to focus in corporate law, and the school is so singularly focused in international public law. While that is an important course of studies, I have continually been disappointed at the lack of alternatives for those who wish to practice international private law. I aspire to study at Ocean Law School because it has many of the prominent programs leading the world and nation in corporate, international, and economic law studies, precisely those legal interests that I wish to pursue.

For the first time in my life I have focused all of my effort, time, and intensity into my academic studies, and only those. Throughout high school and both undergraduate and graduate school, I was required to balance my academic studies with working full time (in college) and participating in what may have been too many extracurricular activities. Finally—during my first year of law school—I focused entirely on my studies. I am very happy that I did, for this was time well spent. In addition to the great grades that I've earned for my first year subjects, I've loved nearly every minute of it. I've wanted to be a lawyer for years, but was wary of the "law school experience," having heard the traditional horror stories. After living through one-third of the experience, law school is precisely where I belong.

I am a first-generation college student, let alone pursuing Master's and law degrees, who comes from a military background. My parents both served in the United State Air Force, following the footsteps of both of my grandfathers and most of my extended family. I have learned an immense amount of work ethic and respect from my parents, but also the lesson that anything that I wanted was within reach. I have taken this message with me my entire life, and it's driven me to be the strong, independent, ambitious person that I am today. I've overcome many obstacles to be at the top of my law school class—most significantly growing up in a relatively poor financial situation, constant moving around to different Air Force bases, and lacking any family and friends who were attorneys or other professionals to help guide me through graduate and law school. I worked full-time to get through school, took out loans where I needed to supplement my wages, and have earned everything that I've gotten along the way. I am very proud of my accomplishments and will continue to succeed due to the values instilled in me by my hard-working parents.

I will be a great asset to Ocean Law School because I have come from a different background than many law students and have a fresh perspective on many facets of the world. I have a Master's degree in International Business, have studied international economics intensively, and have studied abroad three times in five countries. I hope to combine this extensive business study with that of the law to ultimately pursue a career in international business law.

Many different aspects of business law fascinate me and I am anxious and excited to continue my legal studies so that I might discover in exactly which niche my passion lies.

Please consider my application for transfer admission because I will make great contributions to the intellectual atmosphere at Ocean Law School and am eager to be a part of Ocean's forward-thinking movement in business and international law.

For your statement, focus on what has been important to you, and be sure to be upbeat and positive in all aspects—even where you might not have such thoughts about, say, your first-year program or law school. If it's negative, it really shouldn't be there.

APPENDIX B:
SAMPLE LETTERS OF RECOMMENDATION

Here are two samples of letters of recommendation, which are included here to guide you in the points that law professors tend to cover—and admissions deans and committees expect to see.

If you're asked to help in the drafting of a letter, you should not simply copy what is in these letters. Rather, you should adapt and fine-tune your own suggestions based on your background, experiences, and qualities. If a dean or committee sees a letter that looks suspiciously like another letter they've just read, chances are that will not be a positive for your application. Thus, please take these in the spirit intended: to provide two samples that exemplify points often included in these letters.

Here is the first sample:

May 23, 20xx

Law School Admission Council
662 Penn Street
P.O. Box 8508
Newton, PA 18940-8508

Re: Letter of Recommendation for Gary D. Gunner III

To Whom It May Concern:

Mr. Gary D. Gunner III, a student at Big South College of Law, is seeking admission as a transfer student to your law school. Mr. Gunner was my student in Constitutional Law I this past semester. Mr. Gunner received an "A-" in my class. His LGPA after the first semester of Law School was 3.86. Although all the grades are not in for the spring semester, thus far, Mr. Gunner has earned an "A-" and an "A." The Law School adheres to a strict grade curve. Therefore, Mr. Gunner's grades are hard-earned, do not reflect grade inflation, and put him at the very top of his class.

Mr. Gunner is the quintessential "come-back kid." Due to a knee injury in high school, the hope of attending undergraduate school on an athletic scholarship was lost. Despite that injury, as a sophomore, Mr. Gunner was a member of the East State University men's basketball team. Against the odds, Mr. Gunner, not tall by basketball standards, was on a "Division 1" team, playing with NBA-bound athletes. His class performance evidenced those traits he learned from sports: tenacity, determination, and a commitment to excellence. An energetic student, Mr. Gunner was always prepared and actively participated in class discussion. He raised thoughtful and intelligent questions and added greatly to the classroom environment.

Mr. Gunner is more than an excellent student with a strong work ethic; he has good character and integrity. Like the team-player he was in basketball, he never used his superior talents or past successes to make his classmates feel inferior. Unless his fellow students followed college basketball, no one knew about Mr. Gunner's experience as an East State University basketball player. He did not succumb to the super-competitive mentality typical of so many law students at the top of their class. Most probably, the lesson he learned from competitive sports was to set a standard of excellence for himself, regardless of others' performance.

I have no doubt that Mr. Gunner will be successful in the practice of law. He is a model law student who adheres to the highest standards of professionalism and ethics in his classroom demeanor and his interactions with faculty and peers. He will be a valuable member of your law school community and someone who the profession will be proud to welcome. I wholeheartedly recommend Mr. Gunner for admission as a transfer student to your law school.

                Sincerely,
                /s/ Susan Smith
                Professor Susan Smith, JD, LL.M.
                Associate Professor of Law

Letters of recommendation from law professors teaching one of the six substantive areas of law (Contracts, Torts, etc.) are preferable.

For many students, however, it's not uncommon that a legal writing instructor has a more in-depth knowledge of your skills and traits, and so is a possibility. If so, you should still have a full or associate professor, as opposed to an assistant professor or instructor, write your other letter(s) of recommendation. With that in mind, here is a second sample:

> From the Desk of
> Timothy Q. Timekeeper, J.D.
> Assistant Professor, Legal Methods

April 1, 20xx

Letter of Recommendation: Ms. Arlene Able

To Whom It May Concern, it is my pleasure to provide this letter of recommendation for one of Westville University's excellent students. Ms. Able is currently enrolled at the College of Law in Chincy, Missakansas. She has demonstrated excellent analytical and reasoning abilities. In addition, she is able to communicate her understanding of the law in a manner that is both instructive and understandable. Her academic achievements are well documented. It is these abilities, and others, that make her an asset as a member of the legal community.

There are personal characteristics of Ms. Able that are exemplary. Ms. Able has been attentive to the needs of her fellow students in assisting them in their continued preparation at law school. She has been supportive in her relationships with other students by assisting them in gaining an understanding of law school course work. She is professional in her conduct, at all levels, with fellow students and her faculty.

It has been my pleasure to have Ms. Able as a student. The mechanics of teaching become much more manageable when students are prepared and participatory. Ms. Able will be a welcomed addition to the legal profession.

If I may provide any additional information or assistance please do not hesitate to contact me.

Respectfully,
Timothy Q. Timekeeper

Appendix C:
Sample Résumés

Jacques P. Johansson
123 45th Street, Washington, D.C. 20002 – (123) 456-7890 – p.p.johansson@gmail.com

EDUCATION

U.S. University College of Law   Washington, DC
Juris Doctor, Expected Graduation – May 2010, Top 5%
  Honors: Legal Rhetoric: Research & Writing: A; Highest Grade Distinction: Contracts, Property
  Activities: Integrated Curriculum Dean's Fellow & Administrative Assistant, *U.S. University Law*
  Review, Women's Law Association, Phi Alpha Delta Legal Fraternity
  Study Abroad: European Comparative Law Program *May-June 2008* London, Paris, Geneva

University of America   Collegetown, USA
 Master of Arts in *International Business – August 2007, with honors*
  Thesis: A Volkswagen Case Study: Paternalism, Positioning and the People's Car
  Honors: Certification in Global Management, Blue Key Honorary Leadership Fraternity
  Activities: Worked full time to finance education
  Study Abroad: University of New South Wales *February-July 2007* Sydney, Australia
   Australian Corporations Law; Geopolitical Risk Mgmt.; Global Banking Mgmt.
 Bachelor of Science in *International Economics*, May 2006 Collegetown, USA
  Honors: University Honors Program, 2005 Homecoming Court Top 5 Finalist
  Activities: Worked full time to finance education, Panhellenic Counselor, Kid's Day Director
  Study Abroad: American Institute for Foreign Study *January-May 2006* Rome, Italy

EXPERIENCE

US Department of State, Washington, DC   June 2008 - present
 Full-time paid Legal clerk, Office of International Claims and Investment Disputes
  Accepted position to conduct international legal research and writing about investment disputes
  concerning NAFTA, the US-Iran Tribunal, and international torts against the US.

University of America Performing Arts, Collegetown, USA   Aug. 2006 – Feb. 2007
 Director's Intern and Intern Coordinator
  Assisted the Director in administrative duties and programming for the Performing Arts Program;
  acted as liaison between student organizations and University of America Performing Arts; managed
  all interns and served as liaison with supervisors; helped develop and structure the intern program.

University of America student government, Collegetown, USA   Aug. 2003 – May 2006
 Budget and Appropriations Chair and Student Senator
  Allocated $12 million Student Activity and Service Fee funds to administrative entities; conducted
  Activity Fee, Organizational and Special Events Budget Hearings; acted as liaison between Budget
  Committee and all student organizations; authored bills to improve the welfare of constituents.

Alpha Alpha Alpha Sorority, Collegetown, USA   Aug. 2002 – May 2006
 Vice President of Finance and Treasurer, Alpha Psi Chapter
  Managed the $1 million+ budget for the chapter; created all officer budgets and oversaw all spending
  of monies, including accounting and audits; maintained relationship with national organization.

The Wetlands Restaurant, Collegetown, USA   Aug. 2004 – Feb. 2007
  Worked full-time in undergraduate and graduate school; served as "shift leader;" managed servers
  and payments; operated as server trainer; handled receipts and all server monies.

ADDITIONAL INFORMATION

  Proficient in *Spanish*; City Collegetown, USA Sungoddess Court Ambassador, Emerging Leaders
  Conference Leader, active Triathlete, scuba diver, and avid world traveler.

Frederick Fauntleroy
234 56th Street, Washington, D.C. 20002 – (203) 456-7890 – fred.fauntleroy@gmail.com

EDUCATION

University of South Carolina   2007 (Spring Semester)
The Dickinson School of Law, Columbia, SC
GPA: 3.79 (Top 3%, Spring Semester)
Honors: **CALI Award-** Legal Research and Writing.

University of Heidelberg, Heidelberg, Germany   2006 (Spring Semester)
Audited courses while on a Fulbright Scholarship

University of Texas at Austin, Austin, TX
Bachelor of Arts, magna cum laude, May 2005
Major: Political Science
Minor: German
GPA.   3.7
Honors: German language scholarship
Activities: University of Dallas Rugby Club – Co-Captain
              University of Dallas Varsity Men's Soccer
              Politics Club
Study Abroad: Rome, Italy, Fall Semester 2002

EXPERIENCE

Fulbright Scholarship, Berlin, Germany   September 2005 - June 2006
- Worked as an English teaching assistant at the Berlin Gymnasium (high school).
- Organized and taught classes ranging from grades 5 to 13
- Organized and coached a high school basketball program
- Tutored German high school students in English

Johnson & Jordan Law Firm, Dallas, TX   May - August 2004
Internship, File Clerk
- Filed and reviewed cases for the firm
- Assisted staff in various duties as assigned

LANGUAGES

- Fluent in German

ACTIVITIES AND INTERESTS

- Fly Fishing, Golf, Skiing, Tennis, Basketball, Soccer, Rugby

Appendix D:
Sample Grade Appeal

Here is a sample grade appeal that one of us used, unsuccessfully, in challenging a 1L grade:

Grade Appeal: Spring 2008 Legal Methods Section 101

This is an addendum to my appeal of the C+ grade I received in the Spring 2008 Legal Methods class section 101, instructed by Professor Jones. According to page 29 of the Bayeast College of Law Student Handbook, "The purpose of this appeal process is to provide a student an opportunity to appeal a grade considered inequitably awarded because it involved a gross violation of the instructor's own specified standards." It is my contention I received a grade in this class that is not representative of my work, because of a gross violation of Professor Jones' own specified standards through the act of another professor grading my final Appellate Brief.

Regardless of the events that took place leading up to my Appellate Brief being graded by another professor, the Brief was written in anticipation of Professor Jones being the sole evaluator of the Brief. Professor Jones made clear specific points on style, structure, and use of authorities, which differed from the universal local rules, that she would deem acceptable and preferred in spite of the teachings of the rest of the Legal Methods classes which included but are not limited to:

- Length and placement of Standard of Review on the same page as the Statement of Jurisdiction

- Short form citations that she considers acceptable

- A concise statement of the facts that did not elaborate on information that was not relevant in advancing one's argument

- The TREAT style of writing in which she wanted to us to illustrate our issues, explanations, and application of the law

- The use of law review articles as persuasive authority in our application section to further our argument

Per a meeting with Professor Klingon and Professor Romulus on July 11, 2005 at 11:00 a.m., it was brought to my attention the standards set forth in grading not only my Appellate Brief but those of my classmates as well. At this meeting, Professor Klingon detailed how she and the rest of the Legal Writing Department determined a standard to grade by. While developing the standard, there was no communication between the Legal Methods Department and Professor Jones regarding any deviations from the standard that she would permit while evaluating the Appellate Briefs.

Thus, none of the aforementioned points discussed above could have been known by the other evaluators except Professor Jones; therefore, any other evaluator other than my professor could potentially penalize a student for following the instructions set forth by the anticipated evaluator's (Professor Jones') instructions, and a student who did not follow instructions by Professor Jones would have benefitted by not being docked points since the Appellate Brief was not graded by Professor Jones.

It is my firm contention the standard used to grade my Appellate Brief had a detrimental effect to both my Appellate Brief grade and my final grade in the class, and that standard grossly deviates from the standard set forth by the intended audience (Professor Jones) of the Appellate Brief.

I move this committee for a grade change and/or if one cannot be decided upon, an "S" grade for the class noting that I have passed the class. Please feel free to contact me if necessary. I can be reached via email at KevinB@urmail.com and/or by telephone at (202)444-5206.

Thank You,

Kevin Bentham
BAYEAST ID# 98765-432

About the Authors

Andrew B. Carrabis played collegiate NCAA baseball and, after graduation, worked as a high school teacher. He earned an MBA from Lynn University and an Executive Certificate of Negotiation from the University of Notre Dame. Andrew completed his 1L year ranked third out of 137 students at Florida A&M University College of Law. Andrew served as an intern clerk for the Honorable Paul G. Hyman, Chief Judge with the United States Bankruptcy Court, Southern District of Florida. He subsequently transferred to the University of Florida Levin College of Law, where he served as the Editor-in-Chief of the *Journal of Technology Law & Policy,* Executive Research Editor for the *Florida Journal of International Law,* and Executive Articles Editor for the *Entertainment Law Review.*

Seth Haimovitch played basketball and graduated with honors from the University of Florida with a Bachelor's degree in Sport Management, where he also earned a Master's degree in the same program. Seth completed his 1L year ranked second out of 137 students at Florida A&M University School of Law. He subsequently transferred to the University of Florida Levin College of Law, where he served as a research editor for the *Entertainment Law Review.*

CONTRIBUTORS

We wish to extend a heartfelt thanks to the following individuals for their kind agreement to offer interviews and narratives, which have added tremendously to this effort:

Robert Brayer completed his 1L year ranked fourth out of 200 students at the University of Florida Levin College of Law. He subsequently transferred to the University of California-Berkeley (Boalt Hall) School of Law, where he received his J.D. in 2002. Brayer practices with Haberbush and Associates in Long Beach, California, where he focuses in bankruptcy and general business litigation.

Kari A. Mattox is the Assistant Dean of Students at the University of Florida Frederic G. Levin College of Law. Mattox is a graduate of the Florida State University College of Liberal Arts and Sciences and the Frederic G. Levin College of Law. She is currently a doctoral candidate in Higher Education Administration at the University of Florida, where she focuses in higher education law and educational leadership and policy.

Jacqueline Pace earned a bachelor's degree in international economics from the University of Florida and a Masters of International Business from the University of Florida and the University of New South Wales in Sydney, Australia. She attended her first year of law school at American University, where she finished in the top 5% in her class of 400 students. She subsequently transferred to Harvard Law School.

Edward G. Tom is the Assistant Dean for Admissions at the University of California-Berkeley (Boalt Hall) School of Law. A native of Salinas, California, Mr. Tom is a graduate of the College of Letters and Sciences and the Graduate School of Education at UC-Berkeley. He has worked in law school admissions since 1975. He is a recipient of UC-Berkeley's Distinguished Service Award and the Excellence in Management Award.

Jason Wu Trujillo is Senior Assistant Dean for Admissions and Financial Aid at the University of Virginia School of Law. As a student there, he was president of the Public Interest Law Association and co-founder and co-president of Voz Latina (now known as the Latin American Law Organization). He was also elected to the Raven Society. Upon graduation, he was appointed an assistant Bergen County prosecutor, serving first in the Appellate Section and then in the Domestic Violence Section. Trujillo returned to the University of Virginia School of Law in 2003 as the director of public service, a role in which he concentrated on job-placement efforts with federal, state, and local government entities, the military, and criminal law positions with both prosecution offices and public defender organizations. He administered the judicial clerkship program and the Virginia Loan Forgiveness Program. In 2004, Trujillo was appointed director of admissions. In 2007, Trujillo transferred to the Dean's Office as assistant dean. In 2008 he was named senior assistant dean for admissions and financial aid.

Neil Wehneman earned a bachelor's degree in Information Systems from the Fisher College of Business at The Ohio State University. He spent his first year of law school at the University of Cincinnati College of Law, where he finished in the top 10% of his class while recording the *Life of a Law Student* podcast. He subsequently transferred to the Indiana University School of Law at Indianapolis, where he graduated *summa cum laude.*

GLOSSARY

1L	A first-year law student, made popular by the 1977 book *One L,* by Scott Turow, about his first-year experiences at Harvard Law School.
2L	A second-year law student.
3L	A third-year law student.
T14	A law school ranked in *U.S. News and World Report's* annual rankings as among the top 14 law schools in the United States. A T14 law school is also often referred to as a "national law school," as its graduates are sought by employers nationwide.
T1	A law school ranked among the top 50, or in the first of four tiers of law schools. A T1 law school (and especially one ranked between 15 and 25) can sometimes be referred to as a "quasi-national" law school.
T2	A law school ranked between 51 and 100, or in the second-highest tier of 50 law schools.
T3	A law school ranked between 101 and 150, or in the second-lowest tier of 50 law schools.
T4	A law school ranked among the bottom 50 of the approximately 200 ABA-approved law schools.
Accreditation	Law schools in the United States are accredited by the American Bar Association. There are three levels of ABA accreditation: accredited; provisionally accredited; and not accredited. Accreditation is primarily a binary consideration, but even accredited law schools are judged relative to other law schools vis-à-vis the quasi-official ranking system described above.

Accreditation (Continued)	A student who enters a provisionally accredited law school is permitted to sit for the bar exam in the state in which the school is located; other law schools might not respect the academic qualities of such a law school, however.
	A student attending a law school not accredited by the ABA will usually face restrictions against taking the bar exam (as only a few states allow such a graduate to sit for the bar exam in their state), and will likely face prejudice from admissions committees at accredited (and especially at higher-ranked) law schools.
Addendum	A supplemental statement to clarify or expand upon an element of an application.
Bidding	A process by which law students request on-campus interviews, often with Big Law firms.
"Booked"	The highest grade in the class. Sometimes referred to as "Am Jur'ing" the class. At some law schools the student will receive a plaque and be reimbursed for the cost of their textbook.
Boutique	A law firm that specializes in an area of practice, such as criminal defense or entertainment law, or that is a "spin-off" firm with partners originally from a larger firm. These firms, while smaller, can approximate the culture and benefits of a larger firm.
The Curve	A bell-shaped apportioning of grades, wherein 50% of the class falls above the median GPA and 50% of the class below it.
GPA	An applicant's undergraduate grade-point average.
Grade-on	At some law schools, admissions to the law review or journal(s) based on grades alone. Often, there is a joint grade/write-on component.
Gunner	A student who talks frequently in class, often engendering negative reactions among fellow students.

Lateral Transfer	Transferring to a law school ranked similarly to the 1L school, often for personal rather than career reasons.
Letter of Academic Standing	The 1L law school's confirmation that there is no academic or disciplinary action against a student. Required by the 2L school and produced by the 1L school's Registrar's office, this usually includes 1L class rank.
LSAC	Law School Admissions Council
NALP	The Association for Legal Career Professionals. Their website, www.nalp.org, assists students in researching potential employers.
OCI	On-Campus Interviews, conducted by employers traveling to limited number of law schools for summer associates, primarily after the second year of law school (and, at T14 schools, after the first year as well). These summer associate positions are usually requisite for a full-time job upon graduation.
Rolling Admissions	Admission of applicants as files are completed, as compared to a process whereby applications are reviewed only after a certain deadline has passed.
Write-on	Competitions held for law journals, usually before or at the beginning of the Fall semester.

GLOSSARY II

Here are terms that are commonly used in the Yahoo Transfer Group, mentioned in Chapter 2. As it can be frustrating to read acronyms that are obvious only after someone explains them, here are some that might save you some of that frustration:

Big Law	A job with a prestigious, national law firm, generally requiring at least 2,000 billable hours per year in a firm with at least 75 attorneys, and a starting salary at or near the top of all salaries nationally.
BU	Boston University School of Law
BC	Boston College Law School
Boalt	University of California-Berkeley (Boalt Hall) School of Law
"Ding"	Getting denied admission.
EA	Early Action, or the process of applying as a transfer student to a law school after receiving only Fall grades.
	Two well-known schools that offer early action admission are Georgetown University Law Center and Washington University of St. Louis.
FSU	Florida State University College of Law
GULC	Georgetown University Law Center
GW	George Washington University Law School
HYS	Harvard, Yale, and Stanford law schools, often grouped together because their admission criteria are comparable.
HLS	Harvard Law School
JMLS	John Marshall Law School (Chicago)

LOR	Letter of Recommendation
LS	Law School
MPbV	Michigan, Penn, Brown, Virginia.
NUSL	Northeastern University School of Law
PT	A part-time law program.
PWL	Preferred Waitlist
Rising 2L	A student who has completed the first year and has not yet begun the second year of law school.
TMSL	Thurgood Marshall School of Law
UGPA	Undergraduate Grade-Point Average
UChicago	University of Chicago Law School
UF	University of Florida Levin College of Law
UM	University of Miami School of Law
UMich	University of Michigan Law School
WUSTL	Washington University of St. Louis Law School
WL	Waitlist

INDEX

OTHER BOOKS

Grains of Golden Sand: Adventures in War-Torn Africa,
by Delfi Messinger
Hardcover 978-1-888960-35-8,
391 pages, US$21.95
Softcover 1-888960-33-4,
391 pages, US$15.95

Grab a ticket for the adventure of a
lifetime: meet a woman who protects
rare apes by painting, in blood, SIDA
("AIDS" in French) on a Kinshasa
wall to keep rampaging looters at bay.

Her mission was to save a small group of endangered great apes—the
bonobo (or "sexy" ape)—from the grip of civil war in the heart of Zaire.
She made this her mission, and after eight harrowing years the reader
will be breathless with amazement in her struggles to get the endangered
animals to safety.

Training Wheels for Student Leaders: A Junior Counseling Program in Action, by Autumn Messinger
ISBN 978-1-888960-13-6, US$21.95

A reference for the engaged parent,
founded on the premise that, if given the
opportunity, mentoring, and guidance,
even young children can work together
to solve (and resolve) their own
problems. They can work towards their
own, common, cooperative goals. They
can build genuine self-esteem.

In two very different schools hundreds of students achieved far more than
they, their parents, their teachers, or the administrators ever thought was
possible. This will improve performance and (real) self-esteem, it will
make true counseling possible for overworked school staff, and it will
connect students to their community. Parents should demand this, while
administrators should support a program that produces truly astonishing
self-reliance and self-motivation among students.

The Insider's Guide to Getting A Big Firm Job: What Every Law Student Should Know About Interviewing,
by Erika Finn and Jessica Olmon
ISBN 978-1-888960-14-3, 130 pages,
US$16.95

While law school teaches many things, how to get a law job is not one of them. In law school, the competition for top jobs is intense—and the special needs of law firm recruiters are unknown to law students. This book is an insider's look at the secrets of landing a dream law firm job.

Later-in-Life Lawyers: Tips for the Non-Traditional Law Student, by Charles Cooper
ISBN 978-1-888960-06-8, 288 pages,
US$18.95

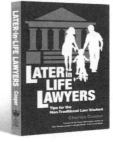

Law school is a scary place for any new student. For an older ("non-traditional") student, it can be intimidating as well as ill-designed for the needs of a student with children, mortgages, and the like. Includes advice on families and children; the LSAT, GPAs, application process, and law school rankings for non-traditional students; paying for law school; surviving first year; non-academic hurdles; and the occasional skeleton in the non-traditional closet.

The Slacker's Guide to Law School: Success Without Stress,
by Juan Doria
ISBN 978-1-888960-52-5, 162 pages,
US$16.95

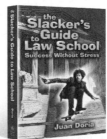

It is easy to fall into a trap of assuming that that one either strives and succeeds or slacks and fails. Enjoying three years of law school is not the opposite of learning the law. There's also a tendency to follow a herd mentality: the assumption that there's just one right way to do something, or just one way to study the law. Too often, this involves too much make-work and too much stress. Do law school right: success without stress. (Or at least with *less* stress.)

For the Law Student

Law School: Getting In, Getting Good, Getting the Gold,
by Thane Messinger
ISBN: 978-1-888960-80-8, 367 pages,
US$16.95

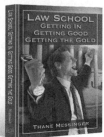

Finally a book for *real* law students. From
the time you decide that law school is for
you, to the process of taking the LSAT and
getting into the right law school, and on to
succeeding in law school and in your
career, this guide will be your silent
companion and mentor. This book focuses
on skills that are readily fine-tuned, with
practical advice that is workable with today's ultra-busy lifestyle.

The key in successful law study is a minimum of wasted effort and a
maximum of results. Still outlining cases? A waste of time. Failing to use
hypotheticals? A dangerous omission. Preparing a huge outline? A dangerous waste of time. Don't waste your time, and don't neglect what's
truly important. Learn law school techniques that work. Once you're in,
Get Good, and Get the Gold!

Planet Law School II: What You Need to Know (Before You
Go)—but Didn't Know to Ask…and No One Else Will Tell You,
by Atticus Falcon
ISBN 978-1-888960-50-7, 858 pages,
US$24.95

An encyclopedic reference for each year of
law school. Examines hundreds of sources,
and offers in-depth advice on
law courses, materials, methods, study
guides, professors, attitude, examsmanship,
law review, internships, research assistant-
ships, clubs, clinics, law jobs, dual degrees,
advanced law degrees, MBE, MPRE, bar
review options, and the bar exam. Sets out all that a law student must
master to excel in law school.

For the New Attorney

Jagged Rocks of Wisdom: Professional Advice for the new
Attorney, by Morten Lund
ISBN: 978-1-888960-07-5, 94 pages
US$18.95

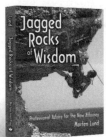

Written by a real-world mentor at a national
law firm, this no-nonsense guide is a must-
have guide for the new associate. Its "21
Rules of Law Office Life" will help make
the difference to your success in the law:
surviving your first years as an attorney, and
making partner. Beware.

Jagged Rocks of Wisdom: Mastering The Legal Memorandum,
by Morten Lund
ISBN: 978-1-888960-08-2, US$18.95

This book focuses on one of the most
complex aspects of professional work for a
new attorney: researching, drafting, and
refining the crucially important legal memorandum. Lund breaks the process of the
legal memorandum into "21 Rules," through
which the mysteries of the perfect memorandum are revealed.

The Young Lawyer's Jungle Book: A Survival Guide,
by Thane Messinger
ISBN 978-1-888960-19-1, 231 pages,
US$18.95

Advice on law office life, including working
with senior attorneys, legal research and
writing, memos, contract drafting, mistakes,
grammar, email, managing workload,
timesheets, annual reviews, teamwork,
department, attitude, perspective, working
with clients (and dissatisfied clients),
working with office staff, using office tools,
and yes, much more.

Recommended in the ABA's *Law Practice Management* and
The Compleat Lawyer, as well as in numerous state bar journals.